How to
Look at
Student
Work
to Uncover
Student
Thinking

ALSO BY
SUSAN M. BROOKHART

How to Look at **Student Work** to Uncover **Student Thinking**

Susan M. Brookhart
Alice Oakley

Alexandria, Virginia USA

1703 N. Beauregard St. • Alexandria, VA 22311-1714 USA
Phone: 800-933-2723 or 703-578-9600 • Fax: 703-575-5400
Website: www.ascd.org • E-mail: member@ascd.org
Author guidelines: www.ascd.org/write

Ranjit Sidhu, *CEO & Executive Director;* Penny Reinart, *Chief Impact Officer;* Stefani Roth, *Publisher;* Genny Ostertag, *Director, Content Acquisitions;* Julie Houtz, *Director, Book Editing & Production;* Liz Wegner, *Editor;* Thomas Lytle, *Creative Director;* Donald Ely, *Art Director;* Masie Chong, *Graphic Designer;* Keith Demmons, *Senior Production Designer;* Kelly Marshall, *Manager, Project Management;* Shajuan Martin, *E-Publishing Specialist;* Christopher Logan, *Senior Production Specialist*

PAPERBACK ISBN: 978-1-4166-2988-7   ASCD product #122011 n4/21
PDF E-BOOK ISBN: 978-1-4166-2989-4; see Books in Print for other formats.
Quantity discounts are available: e-mail programteam@ascd.org or call 800-933-2723, ext. 5773, or 703-575-5773. For desk copies, go to www.ascd.org/deskcopy.

Library of Congress Cataloging-in-Publication Data

Names: Brookhart, Susan M., author. | Oakley, Alice, author.
Title: How to look at student work to uncover student thinking / Susan M. Brookhart and Alice Oakley.
Description: Alexandria, VA, USA : ASCD, [2021] | Includes bibliographical references and index.
Identifiers: LCCN 2020049537 (print) | LCCN 2020049538 (ebook) | ISBN 9781416629887 (Paperback) | ISBN 9781416629894 (PDF)
Subjects: LCSH: Effective teaching--United States. | Reflective teaching--United States. | Active learning. | Professional learning communities.
Classification: LCC LB1025.3 .B7555 2021 (print) | LCC LB1025.3 (ebook) | DDC 371.102--dc23
LC record available at https://lccn.loc.gov/2020049537
LC ebook record available at https://lccn.loc.gov/2020049538

30 29 28 27 26 25 24 23 22 21   1 2 3 4 5 6 7 8 9 10 11 12

How to Look at Student Work to Uncover Student Thinking

Looking at Student Work

Lunchtime. A student teacher and her cooperating teacher, from a self-contained 2nd grade class, are sitting in the school library eating lunches they brought from home. Other teachers are at the table as well. Some conversation can be heard, but not much. Most of the teachers are using the time to catch up on what they call "grading papers." They have between 20 minutes and half an hour, depending on when they are assigned to pick up their students from the cafeteria or recess. The 2nd grade teacher has a particularly tall stack of papers in front of her, so she is grading more than she is eating; she has already asked her student teacher not to bother her. Although she calls it grading papers, she is not really assigning grades to the work. She is marking a check on papers that are completed properly, or mostly so, and circling errors. She is not going to enter this morning's results in the gradebook, just hand the papers back to the students to keep for their Friday take-home packet.

The teacher is grading by herself; she does not seek the student teacher's opinion about the children's work. However, the student teacher is eager to watch and learn so that she knows what to do in the future. Most lunches are like this, her cooperating teacher explains. It's a good opportunity to get through the pile. In 20 minutes, almost a hundred student papers from four different assignments are checked and ready to return. The student teacher did, in fact, learn this approach to looking at student work, and she did the same thing with the work of the 3rd graders in her first teaching position the next year.

That, unfortunately, is a true story. The teacher was a respected member of her elementary school faculty with a reputation as a good teacher. She was not doing anything her colleagues didn't do as well. Grading papers in this manner was standard practice in this school. The student teacher in the story learned that the main reason for looking at student work was just to get through it, and that it was one of a teacher's least enjoyable obligations.

As outsiders looking into that scene, we might have some questions. What, exactly, was the content of the worksheets—did students really have a whole morning of instruction where they were not called on for anything beyond simple right or wrong answers, which might justify this approach? Or was there more information about learning on those pages than the teacher saw, because she was only looking for right answers? Did students' performances on those papers have any effect on the teacher's instruction that afternoon or the next morning? Was this lunch a giant missed opportunity or time wisely spent for the 2nd grade teacher?

Unfortunately, we can't tell you the answers because these are questions we were not asking at the time, and we no longer have those student papers. We do hope that, after reading this book, you come to see student work on well-designed assignments as an important source of information and evidence about students' learning and your teaching, and not as something you need to get through. We're not against efficiency, and we definitely love lunch, but we don't want to miss opportunities.

Student work is the primary means of learning in most if not all classroom lessons and, at the same time, the primary source of evidence about that learning. In their work, students put themselves out there, exposing themselves as learners and as members of the community of learning that is their classroom. Students see their work as an extension of themselves and have a personal stake in teachers' and others' responses to it. Student work is a complex concoction of evidence of student learning, prior knowledge, paying attention, following directions, interest, teacher instruction, and more.

Sometimes teachers look at student work using a simple "who got it and who didn't?" approach. Research shows, and our experience as educators confirms, that many educators look at student work to ascertain its correctness rather than to describe what it shows about student thinking. "Got it/ didn't get it" thinking is summative thinking. "Who got it?" is what you need to know when instruction is finished. Formative thinking is much more helpful for teaching and learning: What did students "get," and how are they thinking about it? What do they still need to understand or be able to do? What next steps in instruction might help students take next steps in learning?

The purpose of this book is to help readers move from looking at student work for correctness to looking at student work as evidence of student thinking. Why might you want to do this? Well, for one thing, it's fun. There is something appealing about students' writing, drawing, and problem solving that was probably one of the reasons you decided to enter teaching in the first place. There are weightier reasons to look collaboratively at student work, as well. The teachers we work with are delighted to be looking at student work because they easily see how central it is to everything they do. Student work showcases teaching and learning in a grounded, authentic manner. In addition, looking at student work collaboratively is a great source of professional learning that benefits teachers and, through them, their students.

The main theme of this book is that looking at student work for evidence of student thinking more than correctness provides more, and more actionable, information for both teaching and learning. In this book, we focus on the student work that results from students' responses to assignments and assessments. That means the student work is partly dependent on student thinking and partly dependent on the nature and quality of the learning goals, instruction, and assignments.

Origins of the Method of Looking at Student Work

Our work in this area builds on a solid foundation of work done by others, both researchers and practitioners. We will describe a few of their projects in more detail in Chapter 5. For now, we want to introduce some of the foundational efforts in this section and highlight some findings in the following section. Then, we will describe our own experience with teachers looking at student work.

Interest in looking at student work can be traced back to at least the school reform movements of the mid-1990s to early 2000s (Little, Gearhart, Curry, & Kafka, 2003). Little and colleagues conclude, "There is something important to be learned by giving close attention to students' experience and students' actual work" (p. 185), and "There is emerging evidence that some versions of looking at student work yield benefits for teaching and learning" (p. 186). They described three projects, based in Harvard Project Zero, the Coalition of Essential Schools, and the Academy for Educational Development, respectively, that used looking at student work as a vehicle for school reform. Common elements of these successful projects included the following: (1) bringing teachers together to look at student work collaboratively as opposed to alone, which is how teachers typically look at student work; (2) focusing on student work, which did not have much of a footprint in professional development; and (3) structuring conversations with protocols to make sure the collaborative talk was a productive way to develop teacher community and school reform. From these school-reform beginnings, protocols took hold as a useful tool for looking at student work (Blythe, Allen, & Powell, 2015) and eventually all kinds of other teacher collaborative activity (Easton, 2009).

From the mid-2000s to the present, the focus of looking at student work has moved from general reform efforts to professional development in formative assessment. For example, Gearhart and colleagues (2006) reported on the Academy Program, in which teams of three to four teachers and one administrator (per team) looked at instructor materials, especially assessments, and the student work that resulted. Dempsey, Beesley, Clark, and Tweed reported on the Assessment Work Sample Method—AWSM, "awesome," get it?—for professional development in formative assessment in middle school mathematics (Beesley, Clark, Dempsey, & Tweed, 2018; Dempsey, Beesley, Clark, & Tweed, 2015, 2016). Cleaves and Mayrand (2011) reported on the Mathematics Learning Community (MLC) project.

The evolution of the movement to look at student work shows two major shifts from earlier professional development methods. First, looking at student work represents a switch from looking at teaching to looking at evidence of learning. That shift requires redefining "evidence of learning" to include evidence of student thinking, not just correctness. Second, looking at student work represents a move to make students, as represented by their work, more central to professional development that has so often involved teachers working on instructional materials without students.

We are excited about both of these shifts, because we think they represent an effective way forward and a way to bring valuable student evidence into the professional development picture. These shifts demonstrate a more general trend toward students and learning that is taking place in both scholarship and practice, especially in the area of formative assessment. As Lee, Chung, Zhang, Abedi, and Warschauer (2020, p. 125) concluded in a review of literature on formative assessment, "Overall, over the past decade, there has been a shift in the focus of formative assessment work from the teacher to the learner." Gradually and sometimes painfully—old habits die hard—both scholars and practicing educators are moving from an "instructivist" approach to education, emphasizing the transmission of content from teacher to student (Box, Skoog, & Dabs, 2015, p. 973), toward a more constructivist approach to education, emphasizing that students construct their own knowledge from exposure to various learning opportunities, as current learning theory states. If students construct their own knowledge, then to be effective, teachers need to know how students are thinking. This impetus toward the formative and the growing acknowledgment that students construct their own knowledge make looking at student work a particularly timely approach to teaching and to professional development.

Demonstrated Benefits of Looking at Student Work

The projects we described above, and some other research, converge on four important outcomes. Research suggests that these four outcomes are improved when teachers look at student work for evidence of student thinking more than correctness:

- Understanding what students are thinking about concepts and skills they are learning.
- Providing effective feedback that feeds student learning forward.
- Deciding on next instructional moves.
- Supporting professional development.

Understanding Student Thinking

Understanding student thinking requires teachers to reason formatively: not just "Did they get it?" but "What did they get?" (Otero, 2006, p. 254). This requires a shift in teachers' conceptions of and beliefs about learning in general, and formative assessment in particular, from the views they often hold when they leave preservice teacher education. Otero's study showed that this shift can happen, but it is difficult, and by no means did all of her preservice teachers get there.

Working with inservice science teachers, Furtak and colleagues (2016) showed that, in professional development using learning progressions to design formative assessment in science, teachers increased their abilities to do many things, including interpreting students' ideas. Kazemi and Franke (2004) documented two changes in teachers' participation in professional development that featured facilitated group examination of student work in mathematics. The first, which occurred early in the project, was a move toward paying attention to the details of students' thinking, accompanied by "surprise and delight in noticing sophisticated reasoning in their students' work" (p. 213). The second change followed from the first. As teachers noticed more precisely the content and quality of their students' thinking, they began to think in terms of instructional trajectories they could use that would build on that thinking.

Heritage and Heritage (2013, p. 176), working with one expert teacher, showed that student-teacher dialogue, with the teacher interpreting student thinking in real time, was "the epicenter of instruction and assessment"—in other words, that being in tune with student thinking is at the very core of clinically effective yet student-centered, relational teaching. Cleaves and Mayrand (2011) showed that teachers' own mathematical content-area thinking improved as they discussed student work, as well.

Providing Effective Feedback

Providing effective feedback requires that teachers understand what students are thinking. Effective feedback does not mean making every possible comment on a piece of student work, but rather suggesting the next steps that would be most useful for students to make progress toward the learning goal in question. Obviously, you can't do that until you know where students are in that learning trajectory—what they're thinking now and what they should experience next. In addition to growth in interpreting student thinking, the science teachers in Furtak and colleagues' (2016) study increased the quality of their feedback after working with learning progressions and formative assessment. The teachers in Gearhart and colleagues' (2006) study reported that as they looked at student work more closely than they had before. One realized she could now give students feedback that they might be interested in (p. 245); another reported she had been forced to realize herself what she wanted every student to know (p. 256), so that she could give feedback that was deeper than "got it" or "didn't get it." For the math teachers who worked with Beesley and colleagues (2018), the greatest area of improvement was in feedback. They improved on two specific measures of the quality of their feedback more than on any of the other aspects of formative assessment measured in the study.

Deciding on Next Instructional Moves

Deciding on next instructional moves is similar to feedback in requiring that teachers understand student thinking and what specific next steps the students should take. It goes one step further, in that teachers must plan and implement lessons where those steps are taken. Otero (2006) showed how making instructional decisions and determining intermediate objectives follows from knowing a student's conceptual understanding at a given point in time. There is some evidence that most teachers, without any special focus on student work, find this very difficult to do (Heritage, Kim, Vendlinski, & Herman, 2009; Schneider & Gowan, 2013).

We have already mentioned that Kazemi and Franke (2004) found that once teachers began to consider student thinking, they moved to considering the implications for instructional trajectories based on that thinking. Steinberg, Empson, and Carpenter (2004) reported a case study of one mathematics teacher whose involvement in understanding students' thinking changed dramatically within the first few months of focusing on the thinking evidenced in students' discussions. Her focus on student thinking became a catalyst for improvements in her instruction that were still in evidence three years later. Those instructional changes centered around facilitating interactive discussions that gave students opportunities to voice and share their thinking and to respond to their peers' ideas.

Supporting Professional Development

Looking at student work is a particularly powerful way to *support professional development*. Windschitl, Thompson, and Braaten (2011, p. 1311) showed that using student work artifacts in an induction program allowed more than one-third of their first-year science teachers to develop the kind of "ambitious pedagogy" usually associated with expert science teachers. The first-year teachers made the most progress in asking students for evidence-based scientific explanations in their work, a practice that grew out of their collaborative experience of looking at student work for evidence of student thinking. As they became more aware of what students were thinking, they in turn were able to work out how to provide more precise scaffolding for their students in subsequent instruction.

All of the studies we have cited in this chapter made the point that bringing student work to the table brings students and their learning into the professional development process—where it arguably should have been in the first place. Another way looking at student work supports professional development, about which we'll have much more to say throughout the book, is that it is a way into professional development for teacher-learners at all levels. All teachers, regardless of their level of content knowledge and pedagogical knowledge, give students work to do and see in that work a reflection of their instruction and their students' learning. Differentiation for different professional learners is built in, as well. Otero (2006) showed that teachers with differing levels of prior knowledge respond to student work with differing levels of depth of interpretation—but they all could and did respond. As teachers' knowledge deepens, so do their depth of understanding of student thinking and the quality of the feedback and instructional moves that follow.

Looking at Student Work with Teachers

Our professional development using student work has been based on Sue's classroom assessment design work (Brookhart, 2017; Moss & Brookhart, 2019) and Alice's expertise in teacher coaching and professional development. As a method, we adopted a professional learning community (PLC) format structured around looking at student work. Alice facilitated the PLCs.

We invited people to participate by choice, to make sure that teachers were interested in the project and did not feel coerced. They could join as grade-level teams or as individuals and had a choice about scheduling. They could attend our sessions before school, during school (by giving up a planning session), or after school. We designed a series of meetings across several weeks so teachers could examine student work, go back and apply ideas, and then meet again. Groups were small, about four teachers each.

To our surprise, we had no problem getting teachers to join in this project. Because time is always limited in schools, we purposefully limited direct content delivery to the first session. There was no time for a workshop, so we started with conversations. The first session was designed to introduce some foundational information about the formative assessment cycle and feedback. Sue provided some materials for this first session, with Alice as the on-site facilitator. The content was just enough to get people warmed up to the ideas and discuss what kind of work would be useful to share with each other. After that, Alice facilitated conversations with each of the PLC groups, approximately weekly. As the weeks progressed, she became more of a coach than a facilitator, as participants shared their students' work and looked at it together.

When we sat down with teachers to look at student work, we noticed something interesting. At the end of the first session, participants were smiling, laughing, even enthusiastic. In fact, the group who met after school had to be ushered out of the building. This was unexpected. When asked, the teachers told us they loved the opportunities to come together. To talk. To have time to think and brainstorm in a professional setting. One teacher commented, "I am so excited to be talking about teaching and learning as opposed to just testing conversations and checking off boxes."

We'll have more to say throughout the book about the teachers we met, their students' work, and the insights they gained. For now, it is simply important to know that our professional development design came out of a growing movement to center professional development on looking at student work and that the examples in this book came from a voluntary project that required teachers to have no particular prior knowledge or experience about formative assessment, just a desire to look more closely at evidence of their own students' learning.

How This Book Is Organized

This first chapter has described four outcomes that have been found to result from looking at student work: inferring what students are thinking, providing effective feedback, deciding on next instructional moves, and supporting professional development. These four outcomes serve as the outline for Chapters 2 through 5. Each chapter will unpack one of these important outcomes for teachers, which connect directly to improved instructional experiences for students. Each chapter also includes a feature called Coach's

Corner, which summarizes insights instructional coaches can use when working with teachers.

The discussion will be illustrated by student work and teacher insights collected from our professional development work. The teachers' and students' names are pseudonyms, but their stories are real. These examples will help readers develop understanding and skill in looking at their own and colleagues' student work deeply and using this evidence of learning effectively. Most of the examples we share are two-sided examples: They include examples of both student work and teacher insights. In some of these examples, the teacher insights were profound for them, even though the student samples on which they are based are simple. The examples illustrate that looking at student work catalyzes teacher thinking as well as illuminates student thinking. Depending on your background and experience, the example teachers may or may not have had the same insights you would have in the same situation. We recommend you use three questions to help you learn from the examples:

1. What does the student work show about the student's thinking?
2. What did the teacher learn, or what decisions did the teacher make, from the student work?
3. And finally, what can I learn from these examples of student and teacher thinking?

Chapter 6 concludes the book by urging readers to begin to look at student work in a new way or continue this journey if they have already begun. The chapter includes suggestions for steps teachers, coaches, and building and district leaders might take to make this happen. We also offer some concluding thoughts of our own. We hope you are ready to join us on the journey.

 ## Reflection Questions

1. How do you usually look at the work your students do? What insights or enhancements to your practice are you hoping to gain from reading this book?
2. Do you have a forum for looking at student work collaboratively with colleagues? If so, what has that experience been like for you?

2

Inferring What Students Are Thinking

Looking at student work with an eye to what it shows about student thinking yields more information than you get from just correcting the work. In addition to finding out whether students were correct, you get an understanding of how they are thinking about the concepts and skills they are learning. This information is also more diagnostic than mere level of correctness—when you know how students are thinking now, it is easier to figure out what they can and should be thinking about next. However, you can't infer thinking that isn't shown in the work.

The thinking students display in their work depends on the nature of the learning goals you are assessing and the appropriateness and quality of the assessment tasks. These things limit the nature and quality of the evidence of learning found in student work. For example, if you ask students to use a word bank to fill in blanks about soil erosion from wind and water, you can infer that they can recognize what goes in the blank. If you ask them to explain how soil erosion works, you may get more information about how they understand erosion works. If you ask them to design a farm that can grow crops on a hillside, you may get information about how they can apply their understanding of erosion to solve problems. Each of these assessments offers different opportunities to get evidence about students' memory, comprehension, and problem solving, respectively. Each gives a different window into student thinking. More than one of these assessments, together, may be needed to reflect the whole of the learning goal.

The inferences teachers make about student thinking, based on their work, also depends on teachers' own content knowledge and their understanding of typical student learning progressions in that content. The clues and cues in student work must be interpreted in light of content-based learning goals. The deeper you understand the content yourself, the more cues you may be able to identify in students' work. The more you know about how students typically learn this content, the better positioned you will be to know what those cues mean about a student's growing understanding and what feedback and further learning experiences would be helpful.

Learning Goals, Assignments, and Student Thinking

The quality of the learning goal and criteria, the richness of assignments and assessments, and the alignment of all three affect how much and what kind of thinking students can demonstrate. All studies of looking at student work of which we are aware addressed this constraint in some way (e.g., Beesley et al., 2018; Cleaves & Mayrand, 2011; Gearhart et al., 2006). By looking at student work, teachers learned that they needed to increase the richness of their assignments and the match of their assignments to rigorous learning goals and criteria. The more student work shows student thinking, the more useful it will be for teachers, students, and learning.

This point may be easiest to illustrate with counterexamples. Consider what student work looks like when writing is taught in a formulaic manner, when mathematics is taught as rote plug-and-chug problem solving, when science is taught as a collection of facts rather than as an inquiry process, or when history is taught as a collection of facts rather than as interpretation of primary sources. Looking at student work in these classrooms will certainly give you some idea of how students have appropriated the formula, directions, or facts they have been asked to memorize or apply, but it won't give you a lot of information about what's going on inside their heads in reference to deeper learning in the domain.

For example, we know a 4th grade teacher who taught students to write persuasive paragraphs using a formulaic approach. The students had to state an opinion as a topic sentence, write at least three reasons for their opinion in the body of the paragraph, and then restate their opinion in a closing sentence. This formula comprised the success criteria the students and teacher used to assess the quality of their paragraphs. There was nothing in the learning goal about the quality of the opinion, the strength or clarity of its expression, the soundness or persuasiveness of the reasons—in other words, the learning goal was about using this "sandwich" style formula for writing a paragraph, not about writing persuasively. Their writing prompt was "Do dogs or cats make better pets?" One of the students wrote this:

Student Work 2.1

My opinion is that dogs are a better pet than cats. I like dogs because they are playful and cute. Also they are the best friends to have. Plus they are cuddly and easy to train. The most important reason I like dogs is because they will bark at anybody the dog doesn't know. Also dogs will bark if their trainer is hurt. Now I hope you will like dogs better than cats now.

Many of the paragraphs from the class were very similar to this one. Looking at this student work, you *can* infer some things about student thinking—but they are things about the student's understanding of dogs (and perhaps the student's own dog)—and possibly, but more of a stretch, that the student knows nothing about cats. The student thinks of dogs as cuddly best friends or as watchdogs. Less clear in the student work is how they understand the actual learning goal of writing persuasively. The paragraph is a listlike enumeration: opinion, reasons, closing. It succeeds in persuading the reader that the author likes dogs and that they can support that opinion with assertions, many of which are additional opinions (playful, cute, friendly, cuddly) or unsupported declarations (easy to train, bark at strangers, bark when trainer is hurt). In other words, the students produced paragraphs using the formula, which we enjoyed reading, but they didn't produce much evidence of learning about persuasive writing. This student didn't consider the condition of cats at all—arguably necessary for comparing dogs and cats as pets. But that isn't the student's fault. The students produced exactly what the assignment asked them to produce and met the criteria they were asked to meet.

In stark contrast to this kind of teaching and learning is what has come to be called *ambitious teaching*. Heritage and Wylie (2020, p. 7) ground their thinking about ambitious teaching in three core ideas: "shared understanding of learning goals, eliciting student thinking, and disciplinary discourse practices." In their eyes, teaching and learning is ambitious when it prepares students to understand the precise concepts and skills they are learning in a discipline, produce work that showcases their thinking, and participate in disciplinary discourse (e.g., thinking and speaking like a writer, mathematician, scientist, historian, artist). We have cited studies that showed looking at student work often leads teachers to realize that they need to increase the richness of their assignments and their match to rigorous learning goals and criteria. We found the same thing in our own work with teachers and will show you some examples in this chapter.

Learning Goals

Learning goals, and the assignments linked to them, come in different grain sizes. State standards and curriculum goals can be fairly broad (e.g., "Writes arguments to support claims with clear reasons and relevant evidence"). Unit goals may be more focused goals that feed into the broader goals (e.g., "Selects evidence that is relevant and persuasive and organizes it logically to support a claim"). Teacher learning objectives within a unit may be more focused still (e.g., "Uses evidence that a reader would find credible, factual, authoritative, and/or emotionally compelling"). Most teachers are familiar with this hierarchy of learning goals.

A learning target for one lesson may be even more focused (e.g., "I can make a strong argument for my opinion on whether dogs or cats are the better pets"). A learning target is a chunk of learning that students and teachers aim for—hence the target metaphor—in one lesson (Moss & Brookhart, 2012). It is expressed as a statement in student-friendly language from the point of view of a student who has not mastered it, developed and evidenced by student work, and made actionable by student-friendly success criteria used to appraise that work. The learning targets form a series of lessons in a trajectory that leads to larger unit/curricular learning goals and eventually state standards.

Student work can give evidence at every level, from single-lesson performances that demonstrate student understanding of a lesson learning target through more complex projects and assignments that show student learning on multiple learning targets or larger learning goals. Assessments, too, can be broader or more focused on the learning goals they are meant to index and, therefore, the evidence of learning that should appear in student work. For example, a culminating project in a unit may be designed to assess one or more of the unit's goals. A class assignment within one lesson may be designed to assess the learning target for that lesson. No matter the scope, better and clearer evidence of student thinking will be available from assignments that are clearly matched to intended goals and well crafted enough to tap the learning goals but avoid requiring unnecessary knowledge or skills that might get in the way of students' performances.

Some of the teachers we worked with started out unaware of the actual standards they were to teach and created assignments that scratched the surface of the standard instead of hitting it fully. This is somewhat understandable. When some states decided to shift away from Common Core State Standards and implement their own versions, not everyone received formal training. Like many teachers, several of the participants we worked with were teaching new grade levels and new content, and in some cases, they were entirely new to the school.

Our conversations helped participants get a clearer idea of what the actual learning goals for their assignments or assessments should be and to what standard(s) they should relate. The starting point for our professional development conversations was always to ask what the learning target, goal, or standard for the work was supposed to be. Teachers without a deep understanding of the standard expressed as much during those conversations. Fortunately, teachers had resources they could access to build their own knowledge around what students should know and be able to do. Bringing copies of standards, accessing online versions, and stating the standards became more of the norm by our last session.

Let us show you an example of a teacher who did understand the learning goals she was teaching, and how she used her knowledge to interpret the students' work.

A Classroom Example on Learning Goals: Kindergarten Informational Text

Looking at student work helped Ms. Griffith align her feedback to the intended learning goals. Her kindergarten class was learning about informational text. Because not all her students were able to read on their own, she had conducted a teacher read-aloud with them. The text was a simple text about bears that included where they lived, photographs of different kinds of bears, and things bears do in the wild.

After reading the text aloud to her students, Ms. Griffith asked the students to identify the main topic and key details. This is a specific goal in kindergarten, and Ms. Griffith wanted individual students to draw their answers because not all her students had mastered writing words. She decided to ask each student to draw two details from the text. In studying multiple student responses, she noticed overall they drew bears, forest, scratching, bumps on their backs, and so on. All of these were examples of students who were giving actual details from the text.

One student drew two bears fighting. One bear was black, and the other was brown. During their conference, the student was able to tell Ms. Griffith they were fighting. On the back of the paper was a brown bear living all by itself. Both details were accurate and aligned with the text. This was significant because this student had not been able to draw or articulate his thinking when a similar task was assigned for fiction text. Ms. Griffith was so excited to see this progress because the thinking the student shared aligned directly with the learning goals she had set for the group, and this was an opportunity to give him much-needed positive feedback. Here is a picture of the first drawing.

Student Work 2.2

In contrast, another student, who is a budding artist, drew two bears on her paper. One bear was scratching his back, and one bear was eating fish. Here is her picture.

Student Work 2.3

These are two things bears do, but these actions were not actually in the text. Ms. Griffith recognized the student was bringing prior knowledge to bear (pun intended!), but these details did not accurately address text evidence. Ms. Griffith used this as an opportunity to give this student feedback on how to use details from the text instead of creating her own when describing key details that support a text's main idea.

Ms. Griffith was able to help both students move forward with learning. She was able to do this because the assignment itself was clear to students and clearly matched with the learning goal of identifying key details in a text. Ms. Griffith kept this learning goal in mind while she examined the work, drew conclusions related to that learning goal, and then used those insights to provide feedback to students. She was also able to bracket artistic ability, a factor not relevant to the learning goal, and appreciate it without using it to sway her judgment of the quality of the student's thinking about details in text.

Success Criteria

Success criteria are the qualities students and teachers should look for in the work. The criteria should be directly aligned with the learning goals and provide evidence of learning, not surface-level features of the work or compliance with directions. Success criteria are attributes of the work that students can hold in mind and use as they work, and on which teachers can give feedback that will advance learning toward the goal. They should be shared with students before their work begins. Success criteria are not scores (e.g., 80 percent correct) or grades (e.g., *B*), with very few exceptions, usually for memory goals like knowing the multiplication facts 0–10. If you find yourself wanting to use a score or grade as a criterion, ask yourself, "What would a student have to understand in order to do this work at the 80 percent level?" The answers to that question will lead you to the true success criteria.

As an aside, we should mention that compliance with directions is important and may be assessed in some way. For example, students may have a list of things to check for (name and date on paper, handwriting is neat, etc.) before they turn in a piece of work. Such things are not success criteria for the learning goals. They give evidence of compliance, not student learning, and should be treated separately from the kind of criteria we discuss in this book.

Poor criteria that are misaligned with learning goals at best do not help learning and at worst harm students. In our first PLC meeting, we illustrated this by having teachers examine two contrasting student work samples from a poetry assignment and the associated rubric. The students had learned that poetry has form and structure and had been practicing with simple formats: acrostic, diamante, and haiku. As a culminating assignment, students were to write one poem in the format of their choice on poster paper, identifying which format they used. One of the student work samples was an acrostic school-spirit poem, with the name of the school down the side and complimentary—if a bit bland—adjectives, one per line next to each letter of the school's name, as the text of the poem. The criteria on the rubric were mostly about following directions and good mechanics and presentation, and this neatly written poem came out looking terrific on those criteria. Every word was spelled properly, although most of the words were simple ones like *nice*.

The other student work sample was an acrostic personal statement. The student put his name down the side and a phrase next to each letter of his name that expressed some aspect of his character. His phrases were appealing to readers, and some of his quirky personality shone through his words. However, he missed a letter in a multisyllable word and did not present the title as directed. His lettering was not as straight as the other student's. This demonstrably better poem fared far worse on the rubric, and the feedback he received was that his poem was not very good, when that was not true. It would never have occurred to him or his parents that the teacher's criteria were the problem, so the judgment that he was not much of a writer would probably stick with him into his future.

We usually use these examples to show how important it is that rubrics contain criteria that look for evidence of learning rather than criteria about following directions or surface-level features of the work. Our PLC teachers also used this sample work to talk about what they noticed and what they could infer about the work in front of them and the learning taking place to consider what feedback to give the student and to consider one next step to keep learning moving forward. Because it was the first session, this was all very informal and in conversational style. Nothing was written down in these sessions other than the participants' reflections at the end.

Through the conversations, we noticed two groups were highly focused on the quality of the work as opposed to its quantity. Despite having little experience with clear success criteria or learning goals, when they looked at the work, these teachers were able to point out how the criteria directly affected the feedback the students received. These teachers seemed to have an intuitive sense of what was wrong and what the success criteria should have been, even though they had not yet been exposed to a more systematic discussion of goals and criteria. Looking at student work drew out these ideas, and the PLC discussion gave participants the time and space they needed to crystallize them.

In this example, the student with the lower-quality poem received more positive feedback. The student with the higher-quality poem received more negative feedback. This bothered the group because they realized that with the wrong success criteria, the wrong things are emphasized in instruction and likely, wrong lessons were learned. After a lively discussion, the point was made that quality matters and the way to increase the quality of student work is by establishing clear success criteria.

Sometimes, students can be involved in co-creating success criteria. This is a great strategy for learning targets with which students have some familiarity. For many of our PLC teachers, including students in this way was a new idea. Teachers had typically decided what students would do each day and how they would be assessed. In our early discussions, teachers shared how they involved students in developing behavioral routines and procedures for classrooms, but they had not included them in developing success criteria related to content learning.

As our sessions progressed, several teachers were very energized by the idea of having students reflect and become part of the learning process. One 4th grade teacher was able to pull her students into the work by having them develop the details on a rubric related to writing in math.

A Classroom Example on Learning Goals and Success Criteria: 4th Grade Math

Ms. Jones is a veteran teacher who is teaching only math this year. She has traditionally taught a 3rd and 4th grade class and loops with her students so she has one class for two consecutive years. She is in the second year of her rotation with these students, and she is teaching 4th grade math. Her 4th grade colleagues teach English language arts, science, and social studies. The school hosts an annual schoolwide Young Authors' Day that is attended by parents and other community members. The school's expectation is that all students will have at least one published piece to share with the audience. For this event, Ms. Jones wanted to design work that would allow her students to deepen their math content understanding as well as develop math writing skills.

Ms. Jones decided on both a writing goal and a math goal for the Young Authors' Day lessons and assignment. The writing goal was that students would improve in their writing of cause-and-effect essays. The math goal was that students would explore the value of a mathematical object used in everyday life to serve some ordinary purpose or solve a problem in daily life (e.g., a calculator). Students were asked to choose a math object and write about what would happen if it "quit" and were no longer available to students. After Ms. Jones gave a few examples, students chose an item to write about and began drafting their pieces. Students started writing, and while things seemed to be moving along, Ms. Jones reflected on ways to make the work even better.

Ms. Jones began looking at the student work as the students were doing it. Her observations led her to realize she knew the success criteria for this assignment, but the students needed to have a better understanding of them. She outlined her project criteria in a skeleton rubric and then invited the students to participate in developing specific criteria to align with these "look-fors." They shared ideas together as a class using what they already knew about writing, and with guidance from Ms. Jones, they were able to build out the full rubric. She said, "I really wanted the students to tell what would constitute a Level 3 (out of 3) on this project. I knew many of them had never written in math like this, and I wanted to allow them to take ownership as writers." These are the shared success criteria that formed the basis of the rubric:

Writing in Math: "The Day the Math Object Quit"

- Clearly identify the math object and explain why it is important.
- Fully explain the cause of the math object "quitting."
- Fully explain the effect of the math object "quitting."
- Write a conclusion that tells whether the math object changed its mind and returned to its job, or not.
- Language mechanics (title, author, capitalization, punctuation).

Because the first draft was under way, Ms. Jones asked students to use their rubric to reflect on their writing. Next, the students used the rubrics they helped create to conduct peer editing conversations. As the writing process unfolded, Ms. Jones was able to see a progression: "They started writing without the rubric in front of them, then once they got the rubric, they wanted to do a lot more work. Then, once they learned it was going to be peer reviewed, they did a lot more work again." Students' involvement in both creating the rubric and using it as they wrote helped them clearly understand what they were working toward. Here is a first draft of one student's essay, "The Day the Numbers Quit."

Student Work 2.4

The Day the Numbers Quit

Numbers are important because without numbers you wouldn't be able to do multiplication, division, fractions, decimals, or number lines. The numbers quit because they were tired of being used. When they quit, they went to another school and at that school the kids hated math. Without numbers teachers wouldn't be able to teach the students and the students wouldn't know any math. So they lived on the streets until number 8 said 'we should go back to the old school because I feel guilty about what we did to the kids?'. All the other numbers disagreed. So 8 went by himself. Meanwhile, the other numbers wanted to go visit 8. When they went back to the school and saw how sad the students were and they realized that it doesn't matter how much they got used everybody needs them. So they went back to the kids and everyone was happy again.

When we left Ms. Jones, she and her students were moving into the final editing and revisions in preparation for the publishing phase.

What can you tell from this essay about how the student is thinking about cause-and-effect writing? We think we see at least three, and possibly four, statements about how one thing caused another. Based on the criteria he is supposed to be using in his writing, what feedback would you give this student that would help him strengthen his next draft? What can you tell from this essay about how the student is thinking about numbers? Does this essay suggest that the student is thinking this is mostly a writing assignment that just happens to be about math or mostly a mathematical problem that needs to be communicated in writing?

The point we are trying to make is that this essay and the student thinking it showcased were partly determined by what the assignment asked for and what criteria the students were using. In school assignments, you get what you ask for! Notice, for example, that this and all the other cause and effect essays were really narratives with cause and effect built into stories instead of expository essays. That is because the prompt—what was asked for—made these young writers think of stories. Notice also that the criteria are clearly reflected in the students' writing.

Looking at student work prompted Ms. Jones's insights that the students needed criteria, and the way she had students participate in drafting a rubric and peer editing drew them into the writing. We think this example also suggests a next step in learning for Ms. Jones. As she noticed that the student work from this assignment was narrative in form, more like stories that happened to be about math than writing within the discipline, she might have decided that the next time she wanted students to do mathematical writing, she would revise the learning goals, edit the writing prompt and rubric, or do both.

The high school teacher in the next example used a prompt that *was* well aligned with the learning goal. However, he did not find the student work that resulted sufficiently deep. As in the elementary example above, the quality of student work revealed the need for success criteria.

A Classroom Example on Learning Goals and Success Criteria: High School Civics and Government

Mr. Miller is a veteran high school history teacher. He has recently had to move his classes online because of the COVID-19 pandemic. In his civics and economics class, students have been learning about the influence of various special interest groups on laws made in the U.S. Congress. The relevant state standard is FP.C&G.3.6 (NCDPI, n.d.): "Explain ways laws have been influenced by political parties, constituents, interest groups, lobbyists, the media and public opinion (e.g., extension of suffrage, labor legislation, civil rights legislation, military policy, environmental legislation, business regulation and educational policy)."

In lessons leading up to a unit assessment, students had discussed several ideas. They learned that political action committees (PACs) are formed to raise money for political campaigns, with the goal of winning elections. They learned that special interest groups hire lobbyists to persuade members of the legislature to oppose or favor bills related to their interests. They learned that special interest groups file lawsuits to challenge existing laws.

One of the questions on the unit assessment read as follows: "Choose a special interest group. Describe the position of this group. Explain one (1) way it can influence the lawmaking process." Here are two students' responses.

Student Work 2.5

A special interest group that I have chosen is PETA. PETA (People for the Ethical Treatment of Animals) is a group that focuses on the protection and treatment of different animals. Certain animals can be close to extinction so they influence their protection by laws so that they are illegal to be hunted/poached.

Student Work 2.6

The National Rifle Association, or the NRA, is an organization whose main focus is protecting the right of Americans to bear arms and defend themselves. They are a largely, if not entirely, republican organization. The politicians they donate large sums of money to are likely to listen to the wants of the NRA and make decisions on bills coinciding with this so that they may keep their funding. For example, a NRA-supported politician would likely abolish gun control.

Mr. Miller noticed that students showed only a surface-level understanding of the concepts. He knew he had taught the material—or thought he had. The question asked the students to identify and describe a group and then explain how that group can influence lawmaking, a question that was in alignment with the standard. Mr. Miller had expected responses that specifically explained how a PAC, lobbyist, or lawsuit could influence the lawmaking process. Choosing and describing a special interest group was the first step. Applying the group's position to the lawmaking process was at the heart of both the standard and the question, and the students did not produce these explanations. They did not describe how the ideology of the group would motivate pressure on lawmakers, explain how the group might exert such pressure, or use the vocabulary they had been learning. Mr. Miller noted Student 2 used a special interest group that had been mentioned in class. He was happy that Student 1 chose a special interest group that had not been previously shared in class. However, both of their explanations fell short of his expectations.

It is possible that Mr. Miller's students really did just have a surface-level understanding of special interest groups and were not capable of writing the explanation in the amount of depth he expected. It is possible that because their class was online, when it previously had been face-to-face, students were feeling more interested in getting work done than in being thorough, a phenomenon he and his fellow teachers had been noticing as learning abruptly switched to online. Most likely, some mixture of these and other factors worked together to result in the cursory answers Mr. Miller received.

Greater attention to success criteria would have been helpful here. Mr. Miller might have collected those things he told us later that he was looking for—identify a group and its ideology, describe how that ideology would make group members want to pressure lawmakers on a specific issue or issues, explain how the group might exert such pressure, and use content-relevant civics vocabulary—and shared them during class lessons on special interest groups. He might have modeled what such explanations looked like in class conference meetings or in written examples and asked students to find evidence of the success criteria in the modeled examples. He might have had students practice writing or videoing their own explanations of the effects of special interest groups on lawmaking and given them feedback based on those criteria.

Teaching online, especially when it comes as a surprise and the transition occurs suddenly, sometimes intensifies issues that come up in in-person instruction. Ms. Jones was able to look at students' work in her face-to-face class as students were doing their first drafts. She realized the need for success criteria and made immediate changes in her instruction. In Mr. Miller's online class, the issue was the same: Students did not realize what a high-quality answer entailed. However, he did not find this out until the end of the unit, when it was too late to do much about it.

Both Ms. Jones's and Mr. Miller's examples illustrated the need for success criteria for student work. Ms. Jones's task did not exactly match her learning goal, however, so most of the evidence she got was about students' narrative writing. Mr. Miller's task did match the learning goal, but students did not have criteria that allowed them to form a clear idea of a quality explanation. In both cases, looking at student work is the way we, and the teachers, discovered these things.

Assignments: Questions and Tasks That Elicit Student Thinking

Questions and tasks that elicit student thinking are generally open-ended in some way and allow for multiple high-quality student responses, not just one correct answer (Brookhart, 2014). To be clear, we are not suggesting that there is no place for questions of fact. Prekindergarten students memorize numbers, letters, their addresses, and all sorts of other things. High school students memorize historical and scientific facts, the names of authors and artists and their work, and so on. What we are saying is that quizzing students on questions of fact does not provide a window into student thinking. It also is not necessary for us to advocate asking questions of fact; teachers do plenty of that already.

The benefits of looking at student work, in the sense we are describing in this book, are best realized when the student work is done in response to open-ended questions or tasks. You are probably familiar with the idea that some questions are open-ended, which means they have more than one possible good answer or several different solutions, and some are closed-ended, which means they have one correct answer or solution.

Performance tasks can be more or less open, as well. Just because something is a project does not mean it is open-ended. Many projects are basically retelling tasks that require only that students look something up and retell it in their work. Consider, for example, what students need to do when their assignment is to report on a planet by presenting a drawing of it (or reproducing a drawing from the internet) and listing facts about it: name, distance from the sun, number of moons, temperature, facts about the atmosphere and planet geology, and so on. In terms of the new Bloom's taxonomy, this might rise to the cognitive level of Remembering, but only if the students actually remember the facts they reported. Many do not.

Now consider what elementary students need to do when their assignment is to plan what future settlers on the planet would need to plan for and do. They would need to report those facts, of course, but also draw some implications from them. In terms of Bloom's new taxonomy, the level of thinking here is Creating. Or consider what high school students would need to do when their assignment is to explain what characteristics of the planet tell about its likely origins, an Understanding-level thinking task in Bloom's terms if they were able to locate this information in science resources.

The trick is not to just pose any old open-ended questions or tasks for students, but to open the parts of the question or task that would lead to evidence of the learning goal. Opening other aspects of a task will not show student thinking in the areas you need to see. For example, we know a high school teacher who assigned her students the task of reflecting on and providing a reader response to Langston Hughes's poem "Harlem." She told the students they could present their reflections as an essay, a rap, or a video. In this case, the core task of reader response was open-ended—multiple student responses are possible—and would give the teacher evidence about how the students were interpreting the poem and making connections to their lives. That evidence is closely aligned to the learning goal. Allowing choice in modes of presentation is fine, and could increase student engagement in the task, but that aspect of openness will not give her evidence about students' thinking about Langston Hughes's "Harlem." Rather, it will give her evidence of students' preference for and facility with a particular medium of expression.

Beware of seemingly open tasks where all of the student choice is in aspects of the task that are irrelevant or peripheral to the learning goal. For example, we have seen student science projects that came from cookbook-style lab manuals, which led to much more evidence of students' presentation skills than evidence of their understanding of experimental design.

One way to think about this is to realize that most tasks have a structure with three aspects: identifying the problem, selecting and using strategies or materials, and presenting the final product (Brookhart, 2014). Each of these elements of the task can be open, guided, or closed. "Guided" in this sense means that the teacher allows student choice from some finite list, like the choice above where students could select to produce an essay, a rap, or a video but not, say, a comic strip. The trick is to open or guide the aspect or aspects of the task that are most directly aligned with the learning goals so that the student work that results will give you relevant evidence of student thinking. In the Langston Hughes example, the learning goal was about interpreting poetry, and the core task was very open ("What is your reader response to the poem 'Harlem'?"). Of course, there are some exceptions to this advice to use open-ended tasks for assessment, but those happen when the learning goal itself is somewhat closed—for example, when high school English students are learning to use MLA style in their papers. In general, open up aspects of questions or tasks that are most closely aligned with, and will give you the best evidence of, student thinking about the knowledge or skills in the learning goal.

Distinguish Between Learning and Doing

In our work with teachers, we learned that teachers sometimes were assigning students things to do without considering what student thinking the task would demonstrate. We acknowledge that a fun task has a certain appeal and may tempt you to think in terms of doing rather than learning. Our advice remains the same: Begin your plans for any assignment or assessment by considering the learning goal. Then, consider what activity or activities might be the best vessel to carry that learning. This increases the likelihood that activities and learning outcomes will be aligned.

If you do find an activity that really appeals to you and want to use it, first consider what appeals to you. It may be that the reason you like the activity is that it does showcase important things you want your students to learn. That's great; your task is now to find where you teach those things and how this activity will fit. Or it may be that the reason you like the activity is not related to one of your learning goals. Perhaps it's fun because it mirrors a popular television show. Then, your task is to adapt the appealing aspects of the activity to a task that does match with an important learning goal in your teaching. In either case, the point is that when you use the activity with students, it will result in student work that will give you evidence of how students are thinking about important learning goals.

Task Quality

In our work with teachers, we also found that identifying the learning goal was not enough: In order to craft rich tasks, teachers also needed to deeply understand the success criteria that the work would need to show. Some teachers continued to struggle with deep and useful understanding of content standards. Even when they identified the specific standard behind their learning goal and read the words, some may not have identified clearly what it should look and sound like for students in their context. For one teacher we worked with, this problem became apparent when she had trouble deciding on how to give feedback to a student. As we backed up and asked her to consider the standard, she discovered the criteria she was looking for in the work had nothing to do with her intended learning goals.

However, it was not all struggle. There were moments of great insight. For example, a 1st grade math teacher reflected, "In foundational grades, we think that the concepts aren't that hard, but we can end up disabling student thinking in the long run if we focus too much on output/fact fluency and not the process and flexibility." When the after-school PLC discussed what they noticed in student work, they used words like *problem solving, inquiry, speaking and listening, collaborative work, thinking flexibly,* and *precise vocabulary.* Their thoughts revolved around what students should know and how they can express what they know. One teacher had the insight that the questions students themselves pose are a source of evidence of how they are making new connections to what they already know.

One 6th grade teacher was able to reflect deeply on how the resources and materials used are a key factor in the student work samples. She came to several important realizations for adjusting the questions and evaluating premade resources prior to using them.

A Classroom Example on Assignment Quality: 6th Grade Science

As a 6th grade science teacher, Ms. Howe recognized the need to differentiate reading selections for her wide range of learners. Her unit related to understanding the Earth/moon/sun systems and was based on state standard 6.E.1 (NCDPI, n.d.): "Understand the earth/moon/sun system, and the properties, structures, and predictable motions of celestial bodies in the Universe."

Ms. Howe selected materials for students to read and asked them to answer comprehension questions with evidence from the text. Ms. Howe regularly incorporates literacy tasks into her science class. By the point in the year of this example, students had written responses to comprehension questions within each unit they had studied. Examining the student work, Ms. Howe noted there was "a spectrum of student responses. I realized the questions at each level are not as clear as I would have liked."

In an effort to differentiate for a wide range of readers in science, Ms. Howe had selected differentiated texts that all addressed the topic of the place and movements of the earth in space. The text at each reading level ended with comprehension questions intended to focus on comprehension of the same concepts but phrased differently. After looking at the student work that resulted, Ms. Howe realized the questions were not necessarily aligned with the standard or readability. Here are some examples of the questions and student responses:

Level A: How is the Earth not the center of everything?

Student Work 2.7

It keeps earth and other planets in place as they go around the sun.

Level B: People used to think that Earth was the center of everything. How were they wrong?

Student Work 2.8

Because the sun is the middle of everything.

Student Work 2.9

They were wrong because we are not the center because the sun is and all the planets orbit the sun.

Level C: Describe Earth's position relative to the rest of the universe.

Student Work 2.10

Earth is one of 8 planets in our milky way and there is 700b billion more! Our planet is only one tiny part in our universe.

Student Work 2.11

Earth's position always changes because it s orbiting the sun. Though, Earth is one of at least eight other planets that travel around the sun. It is located at the edge of the milky way.

Student Work 2.12

The position of the earth is a small spot in the ever expanding universe.

Level D: List three reasons why Earth is not the center of the universe.

Student Work 2.13

The sun is the center. The earth orbits around the sun. Earth is one of the least planets.

Student Work 2.14

It has a tilt. The moon rotates.

Looking at the student work, Ms. Howe realized several important things. She started to notice some students, including her most skilled science students, were taking answers exactly from the text instead of being able to paraphrase and synthesize. This was unexpected, and she eventually attributed this to the way the questions were phrased. To complicate things, she also pointed out that her most needy readers were given a very abstract question ("How is the Earth not the center of everything?"), while her more sophisticated readers had a question that did not dig deep enough ("List three reasons . . ."). This caused her to look at even more student samples to see if the questions really addressed the level of understanding she was searching for.

Ms. Howe decided on two follow-up actions. First, and most relevant to our discussion here about the quality of questions and tasks, she decided she needed to design different questions in order to find whether her students really understood the content. The student work that resulted from the questions she had used indicated only a surface-level understanding of the relationships between the Earth and other planets, the solar system, the galaxy, and the universe.

Second, because of the work samples, Ms. Howe was not sure if the issue was the content or the act of writing about the content. Her second follow-up decision was to create a lesson on how students could put ideas into their own words when responding to science questions. She also felt it would be useful to include a vocabulary review of content-specific vocabulary for students and then use that vocabulary to write to a specific prompt so the answers show more critical thinking and knowledge of the subject. Finally, she decided to create an assessment rubric to bring the expectations into focus for these students.

Ms. Howe's learning, in the words of her own reflection, was "While I am intentionally selecting differentiated reading selections, the questions are not getting to what I am looking for. I need to evaluate all aspects of the text to make sure it aligns with what I am looking for."

This example shows how important the assignment or assessment task is. The question, task, or prompt you use should be designed to elicit the kind of student thinking you hope to find. Students can only respond to the tasks you set for them. If a task does not require the kind of thinking involved in a learning goal, you will not get any evidence of it. This example also illustrates how looking at student work helped a teacher get insights into the quality of the assignment she gave and create a plan to improve her assignments.

Deep Knowledge of Content

Content knowledge and pedagogical content knowledge are both necessary for understanding the student thinking exemplified in students' work (Cleaves & Mayrand, 2011). The more deeply you understand the content you are teaching and the ways in which skilled teachers impart that content to students, the clearer your goals and criteria will be, the more on-point your questions and tasks will be, and the more you will be able to pick up on the clues to student thinking in their work. This is especially apparent in the clarity of a teacher's learning goals and success criteria and in the ability to create rich, cognitively demanding tasks (Dempsey et al., 2015; Gearhart et al., 2006). The old adage about "staying one chapter ahead of the kids" does not serve us well here.

What should you do if you do not feel you have a deep understanding of either the content you are teaching or the pedagogical principles and practices that work well in that learning domain? We have two suggestions. First, these wells of knowledge are learnable, and content learning can be part of professional development that includes looking at student work (Cleaves & Mayrand, 2011). If the content is important to you, you can develop your skills. Second, especially relevant for when you find yourself assigned to teach in content areas where you are not comfortable (e.g., in short-term new teaching posts or long-term substitute posts), consider finding a colleague who does have this expertise and asking for assistance. Or perhaps you can find a colleague with the expertise who needs help in an area of strength for you, and you can collaborate.

In our work with teachers, we found the principle of deep content and pedagogical content knowledge to be especially important for looking at student work. The teachers who had a strong command of the content easily and somewhat effortlessly jumped from looking at student work to feedback and next steps, based on how they understood students' learning trajectories in their content area.

As an example, two of the kindergarten teachers with whom we worked shared student work samples in anticipation of Young Authors' Day. You have already met Ms. Griffith, and you will meet Ms. Fiorenza in the next section. These two teachers were able to share insights on student thinking and consider feedback and next steps much more easily with writing than with reading. In the PLC reflections, we learned that neither one had realized this. Most likely, they each have a deeper understanding of writing pedagogy than reading pedagogy. That insight alone will allow each of them to gather the information and experience they need in kindergarten reading—because now they know they should seek it out.

The following example about deep content knowledge shows how understanding science helped one teacher avoid being distracted by extraneous information in student work and give useful feedback anchored in the science standard. A teacher with a surface understanding of the content may have thought the student understood concepts and vocabulary when he did not. The teacher realized this herself in her reflection. She wrote, "You could look at this and think they are on track but they are not."

A Classroom Example on Deep Content Knowledge: 1st Grade Science

Ms. Sandoval was teaching a unit on the moon. The state standard (NCDPI, n.d.) was 1.E.1.2, "Recognize patterns of observable changes in the Moon's appearance from day to day." Her classroom learning goal for this series of lessons was that students should understand that the moon looks a little different every day, but it looks the same about every four weeks. Ms. Sandoval had explicitly taught students that waxing is "growing toward a full moon" and waning is "getting smaller toward a new moon." The students had been keeping moon charts in addition to the other work they have done around this standard.

The assignment she gave her students in one lesson was this: "Draw the moon from last night and predict what it will look like tomorrow night. Explain your thinking with words." The criteria for successful work were that the shape of the moon in the picture should be a waxing crescent, and the explanation should include what it will look like next. Here is one example of student work.

Student Work 2.15

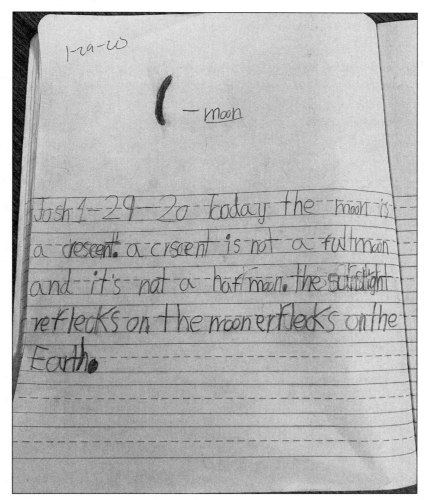

At first glance, you might think this work indicates the student understood the phases of the moon. However, Ms. Sandoval was able to see where there were some gaps. She unpacked her thinking for Alice.

Ms. Sandoval: Look at this. He has concepts in the answer but not what we are looking for. There are some surface components, but he didn't get it.

Alice: Tell me about that. What do you notice?

Ms. Sandoval: The shape is wrong [it's a waning crescent, not a waxing crescent]. He did not talk about what it will look like next. He didn't hit the criteria I was looking for. He does have awareness of difference phases. He pulls on background knowledge—the sun.

Alice: What does the work tell us? What can we infer?

Ms. Sandoval: He understands basic concepts and is aware of vocabulary related to this concept. He doesn't see the pattern as observable or predictable.

Alice: What would your feedback be for this student?

Ms. Sandoval: "I understand you saw a crescent moon. Can you tell me what the moon might look like tomorrow? Why do you think that?" I usually give them feedback as soon as they bring me the paper. I ask them to tell me and then, if they can, they go back and add/change it.

Ms. Sandoval went on to consider the next steps for this student. Based on what she noticed in the work sample, she asked him to watch and chart the moon. She reminded him to use his moon book to practice the sequence. In other words, she used this work sample to decide what to do next for the student.

She said, "I know what I am supposed to teach, but I need to know what they actually know and what they're getting about how it works. I have to pay attention to what the mistake pieces are so we can share both correct information and mistaken information. He has some things in place, but he didn't get it." Thanks to her deep content knowledge, she was able to reflect on content, pedagogy, and assessment without getting sidetracked. She gets beyond the token vocabulary in the written paragraph and is expecting her students to not only be able to notice patterns but also explain them.

Ms. Sandoval's example shows how her content knowledge about the phases of the moon and her pedagogical content knowledge, including what criteria would indicate concept attainment, focused her as she looked at the student's work. The result was deeper clarity about how the student understood the phases of the moon. First, she realized that there was an important difference between a waxing and waning moon, and that not all crescents are the same. We confess that when we first looked at the student's drawing, we thought it looked fine! Our content knowledge was not deep enough. Second, she knew that the difference in crescents was important for predicting the phase that comes next. Finally, she realized that the student's explanation was about concepts he already knew and that evidence of his understanding of the moon phases was missing. A teacher without this content knowledge may well have looked at this student work and interpreted it to mean the student had mastered material when he had not, and the student would not have received the follow-up he needed to move closer to the learning goal.

Learning Progressions

One of the most important elements of pedagogical content knowledge is understanding student learning progressions in key disciplinary ideas. For example, students who are learning to multiply typically understand multiplication as repeated addition before they come to a more multiplicative understanding, such as might be diagrammed in an array. Teachers who know that can look for clues about additive and multiplicative thinking in students' drawings and explanations as they solve multiplication problems.

More generally, learning progressions are successively more sophisticated understandings of a concept over time (Heritage, 2008). Learning progressions describe pathways that students take as they develop in an area of learning. This development is assisted by both instruction and maturation. Learning progressions describe movement from novice to expert performance. Learning progressions are not grade or age based but rather describe movement from less to more sophisticated understanding whenever that happens. Learning progressions help teachers locate student understanding on a path to learning, which is extremely useful, even necessary, for writing targeted feedback and planning strategic next instructional moves (Furtak, Circi, & Heredia, 2018).

The example below shows how Ms. Fiorenza's understanding of how early writing skills develop helped her interpret student work and easily discern next steps for her instruction and her student's learning.

A Classroom Example on Learning Progressions: Kindergarten Writing

Ms. Fiorenza is a second-year kindergarten teacher. She has a diverse group of students who come to her with a wide range of literacy skills. Her students were working on a learning goal based in her state standards:

> W.K.2 Use a combination of drawing, dictating, and writing to compose informative/explanatory texts in which they name what they are writing about and supply some information about the topic.
>
> > a. With guidance and support from adults, respond to questions and suggestions from adults and/or peers and add details to strengthen writing as needed. (NCDPI, n.d.)

Her students used writing journals to record their thoughts and practice their writing. One student had been struggling to communicate through writing. Early in the year, instead of drawing pictures in his journal, he could only scribble using a variety of lines. As the year went on, he was able to add drawings of stick figures to communicate ideas and started to add letters to the drawings, but the letters appeared to be random. By the second half of the year, he had made good progress. Ms. Fiorenza shared the following example. It shows how her deep understanding of early writing development helped her move from looking at the student work to feedback and next instructional moves.

Ms. Fiorenza: Hi, Sarthak, can you read me what this says in your journal?

Sarthak: "Come into my house please. I won't be bored."

Ms. Fiorenza: What would make you not bored?

Sarthak pointed to the "swing" on the planning sheet.

Ms. Fiorenza: What do you want to tell me about the swing?

Sarthak: It will make me not bored.

At that point, Ms. Fiorenza was able to bridge the gaps in Sarthak's writing and support it with language.

Ms. Fiorenza: Oh! If you want to tell me about the swing, I need your sentence to have the word "swing" in it because if you don't say "swing," I don't know there's a swing.

To her surprise, Sarthak went back and rewrote the entire second sentence. It now read, "So I won't be bored, I can swing."

Ms. Fiorenza: Remember, you need to tell me what you're talking about before you tell me anything about it. The reader needs to know what you are talking about first.

This time, when Sarthak went to edit, Ms. Fiorenza didn't have to be as explicit ("say the word stairs") and he was able to do it himself on the rewrite. The third sentence says, "I can use my stairs to my house."

Student Work 2.16

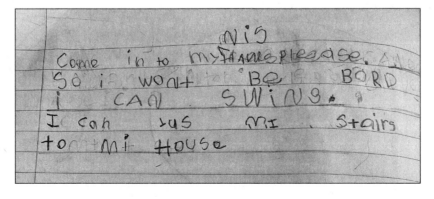

When we reflected on this together, Ms. Fiorenza talked about the progress this student has made in written expression and acknowledged there is plenty of room for growth. Most importantly, she shared that she did not think this student understood the purpose of writing things down. She said he needs to know that "someone needs to be able to read this and understand what you are trying to say." Instead of focusing on spelling, grammar, or structures, Ms. Fiorenza knew she had to go all the way back to the purpose of writing: to communicate. With her gentle feedback and scaffolding of writing learning targets, this student has made progress. Ms. Fiorenza knows that the other parts of writing will come and that, in time, all the standards will be addressed. Instead of rushing the student through content just to cover it, Ms. Fiorenza uses this time to lay the strong foundation and help Sarthak see himself as a writer and a communicator. Recognizing he is still emerging as a writer is the key to moving him along the developmental continuum of writing.

In some topic areas within disciplines, scholars have worked out typical learning progressions and tested them empirically. In many topic areas, this is not the case, and teachers who must plan instruction now cannot wait for future studies. Teaching experience and the wisdom of practice can help here. Teachers who have taught the same learning goals several times often have noticed recurring patterns in students' developing understanding, as shown in their work, and those patterns can serve as expectations for how current students may be expected to develop. As you can see, looking at student work plays a key part in this process. Patterns of thinking evidenced in former students' work suggest expectations for current students' thinking.

 ## Summary

In this chapter, we have shown how looking at student work can give insights into student thinking and meaningful evidence of learning. For this to happen, however, the question or task to which the student responds must be a rich task that is well aligned with a clear learning goal. Both teacher and students need to know what qualities should be evident in the work—the success criteria. Teachers with deep knowledge of the content and typical student learning in that content area are more insightful about student thinking and can move more easily from those insights to providing effective feedback and selecting appropriate next steps in instruction. In Chapter 3, we turn to looking at student work as the basis for providing effective feedback.

Coach's Corner: Hints for Helping Teachers Make Inferences About Student Thinking

- Teachers are often more comfortable talking about student behaviors than content, and they may find it easier to talk about content than student thinking. The coach's role in these conversations is to keep student thinking on the table: Ask questions, listen, validate, clarify, and synthesize information.

- Expect diversity among teacher learners. Suspend judgment so people have room to develop ideas, but guide teachers in the direction of making meaning from looking at student work.

- Do not take for granted that all teachers know their standards or are focused on how to grow all learners. These are keys to looking at student work, however, and may need to be developed.

- On the other hand, some teachers will have deep content and pedagogy knowledge and not only be immediately energized by the discussions, but surprised that others might consider only looking for correct answers.

- People enter into conversations about student work in different places. It is important for coaches to recognize that and create a space for all teachers to contribute.

Explicitly encourage and let teachers take time to point out the things their students do well.

 ## Reflection Questions

1. Look at some work your students have done recently in response to an assignment that you did not think was successful. Can you figure out why that was so? Do the reasons have to do with the things we have shared in this chapter:

   - Clear learning goals and success criteria,
   - Rich tasks that are open-ended in aspects that align directly with the learning goals, and
   - Your content and pedagological knowledge?

2. Look at some work your students have done recently in response to an assignment that surprised you with lots of information about their thinking. How did the following contribute to the depth of inferences you were able to make about student thinking from this work:

   - Clear learning goals and success criteria,
   - Rich tasks that are open-ended in aspects that align directly with the learning goals, and
   - Your content and pedagological knowledge?

3

Providing Effective Feedback

Feedback is most effective when teachers interpret student work in terms of student thinking and use that information to give students insights into their own thinking. When students understand shared learning goals and criteria, they can use the formative learning cycle to play an active part in their own learning. Feedback then becomes advice on these three aspects of learning—instead of just another set of teacher directions or comments—and students are likely to take this advice if they perceive they will be successful.

The Formative Learning Cycle

Formative assessment supports students through a process that is often called the formative learning cycle: Where am I going? Where am I now? Where to next? You may hear that last question phrased as "How can I close the gap?" with the gap understood as the distance between a student's current status and the learning goal. This is a common and helpful way to put it. In this book, we use the more general "Where to next?" to emphasize improvement of any kind, whether or not it takes a student all the way to the stated goal. Of course, the goal is the ultimate destination, but it may take some students several tries to get there. In this book about looking at student work, we want to emphasize next steps more than final mastery.

The formative learning cycle involves students in understanding the goals of their learning and the criteria by which they will understand their current level of progress and their next steps. It involves students in the self-regulation of their learning. The process depends on teachers and students being clear about the goals of learning, both for individual lessons and for longer-term learning, and criteria, as we showed in Chapter 2. Figure 3.1 shows the formative learning cycle in diagram form.

Figure 3.1
The Formative Learning Cycle

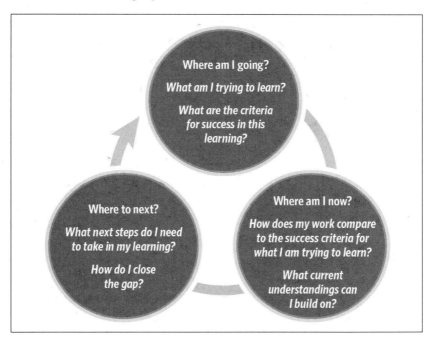

Source: From *The Formative Assessment Learning Cycle* (Quick Reference Guide) (p. 1), by S. M. Brookhart and J. McTighe, 2017, Alexandria, VA: ASCD. Copyright 2017 by ASCD.

As the diagram shows, formative assessment can be most effective when students understand what it is they are trying to learn and what it looks like, produce evidence of their learning, receive formative feedback, and use that feedback to improve. When students understand what it is they are trying to learn, they can more easily activate prior knowledge, focus on success criteria, benefit from feedback, and participate in self-assessment. When teachers structure lessons to support the formative learning cycle, they get insights into students' thinking that help them monitor learning, offer precise feedback, and decide on next instructional moves.

Looking at student work can help teachers understand how the formative learning cycle works. In our work with teachers, we found that having conversations around student work helped teachers naturally discuss parts of the formative learning cycle. At the start of our PLC sessions, most of the teachers were unfamiliar with this cycle. They all brought some sort of student work to subsequent sessions, and the informal conversations inadvertently included where students were trying to go, where they were in this moment of learning, and what would be a logical next step. Alice used the language of the formative learning cycle as she facilitated the group discussion, and teachers easily shared thinking that followed the cycle.

Discussions in all the PLC groups converged on how difficult it is to give students effective feedback without appropriate criteria and how often their learning targets lacked appropriate criteria. Thinking about the formative learning cycle while looking at student work helped teachers who had difficulty with success criteria be remarkably candid and thoughtful. Some admitted they only had a vague idea of what they wanted students to know and be able to do, and some conflated a variety of success criteria into one lesson. Most of these teachers got to the feedback part of the conversation and would say, "I am stuck. I don't know what to say or do with this student." With the student work in front of them, and the problem clearly identified, they were able to back up, look at the standard, examine what would make sense for success criteria, and then move forward with some sort of feedback.

Of course, there were also teachers in our PLC groups who had already crafted and shared appropriate success criteria. Those criteria formed the basis of feedback on student work that would help students move along on the formative learning cycle. Here is an example of how Ms. Hamilton used success criteria with students to help them see where they were going, assess how well they were learning, and provide feedback.

A Classroom Example on Success Criteria and Feedback: Kindergarten Math

Ms. Hamilton was teaching mathematics to her kindergarten students using a state standard under Operations and Algebraic Thinking: Understand addition and subtraction: NC.K.OA.3 (NCDPI, n.d.), "Decompose numbers less than or equal to 10 into pairs in more than one way using objects or drawings, and record each decomposition by a drawing or expression."

For one lesson, she asked her students how many ways they could show the number 5, so their learning target became to show different ways to make the number 5. First, Ms. Hamilton gave pairs of students five red and five yellow chips. With partners, students made combinations like one red and four yellow, two red and three yellow, and so on. After their partner work, students were released to go back to their tables and create the number 5 on their own with visuals. Ms. Hamilton shared these success criteria with her students:

- *I can show the number 5 in more than one way.*
- *I can use objects or drawings.*
- *I can show my thinking with a picture or numbers.*

Luther drew two toys and three snacks. Ms. Hamilton was very pleased with this because in the past he had not been able to represent addition or subtraction accurately. She used the language of the success criteria to frame her oral feedback: "What you did was great. I can see you understand one way to make 5. Can you keep thinking about this and show another way on the back?" That is, she affirmed that Luther had met one of the criteria (using drawings) and made a suggestion so he could reach another one (show 5 in more than one way).

Student Work 3.1

Robert, another student who was struggling with addition, drew what looked to be five cookies at the top of his paper and another five at the bottom. When Ms. Hamilton talked with him, he clarified that three were chocolate chip cookies and two were sprinkle cookies, and the same for the ones at the bottom (four chocolate chip and one sprinkle). Ms. Hamilton anchored her feedback in her success criteria and said, "That is great thinking. I can see you were able to use your chips and show your thinking. Remember you can go back to those anytime you need them. Drawing a picture seemed to help you understand different ways to make 5. Do you think you could do that next time, too?"

One of our favorite aspects of this story is that Robert's work shows he was also using the success criteria himself. He did show the number 5 in more than one way, and he did use drawings of objects—different kinds of cookies. He is very likely to understand what he has learned, understand Ms. Hamilton's feedback, and be able to do it again.

Student Work 3.2

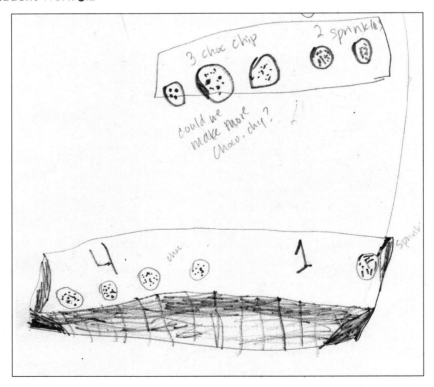

Ms. Hamilton's clear criteria made a ready framework for her feedback to both Luther and Robert, and in fact to all her students. Because she had that *clear frame of reference, she was able to compare students' work with criteria, talk with them, and help them move forward with learning this concept. In other words, because Ms. Hamilton understood the formative learning cycle and used clear criteria, it was easier for her to look at her students' work and give quick oral feedback, and it was easier for her students to understand the feedback and use it to improve.*

This example illustrates how teachers can use the language of success criteria to decide on what to say or write for feedback. This makes giving feedback more efficient because you are not starting from scratch each time to decide what to say. It also makes feedback more effective because if the students are already using those same criteria, they should be able to connect with the feedback more easily than they would if the feedback were new remarks.

Here is an example of how this same principle might look in high school mathematics. For this example, we use some anonymous student work samples because our PLCs did not include a high school mathematics teacher. In these examples, you can see that the principle of using success criteria to look at student work and provide feedback applies at all grade levels.

A Classroom Example on Success Criteria and Feedback: High School Algebra

Algebra students have already learned basic strategies for setting up and solving equations. To extend and apply that knowledge, an algebra teacher wants students to learn that algebraic equations can be written to address word problems, and then the solution to the equation helps solve the word problem. The teacher shared the following learning target with students: "I can use algebraic thinking to model and solve a real-world problem." The lesson and the assignment emphasized three success criteria, also shared with students:

- *I can set up a model that reflects the problem scenario.*
- *I can accurately solve my equation.*
- *I can explain my work.*

Here is one of the problems students worked on in class:

One plan for a state income tax requires those persons with income of $10,000 or less to pay no tax and those persons with income greater than $10,000 to pay a tax of 6 percent only on the part of their income that exceeds $10,000.

A person's effective tax rate is defined as the percent of total income that is paid in tax.

Based on this definition, could any person's effective tax rate be 5 percent? Could it be 6 percent? Explain your answer. Include examples if necessary to justify your conclusions.

Show your work and explain your reasoning. You may use drawings, words, and numbers in your explanation. Your answer should be clear enough so that another person could read it and understand your thinking. (NAEP Released Item 1992-12M12#9)

First, let's look at an example of student work that was well done.

Student Work 3.3

$$X = income$$
$$.05x = .06(x - 10000)$$
$$.05x = .06x - 600$$
$$x = 60000$$

Tax rate is 5% for this income

$$.06x = .06(x - 10000)$$
$$.06x = .06x - 600$$
$$0 = -600$$

No - rate. Can't be 6%

Source: NAEP Released Item 1992-12M12#9.

Feedback for this student might simply be naming and noticing what the student did well, according to the criteria: This student accurately set up an algebraic equation (the model), solved it correctly, and explained the work. The mathematical thinking is mostly communicated in the step-by-step execution of the solution, and the student adds a few final words of explanation at the end. Your feedback might be something like this: "You have written two equations that model the two parts of the problem, and you have solved them accurately. Your thinking is organized and clear." This is so much more informative to a student than a comment like "Great job!" Now the student knows that you noticed what was done well and that it matched the concept being learned. If the feedback is oral and the length of comments is not much of an issue, you might add a thought question. It could be about something that comes next in the learning trajectory—for example, "Do you think there's a way to describe effective tax rates over a range of incomes?" Or it could be something more metacognitive, about how this student might have thought about this problem—for example, "Before you did the second part of the problem, did you suspect the answer [to the question of an effective tax rate of 6 percent] would be no?"

Now, let's look at an example of a student who worked hard on the problem and managed to solve the first part using a guess-and-check strategy, which did not work well for the second part of the problem.

Student Work 3.4

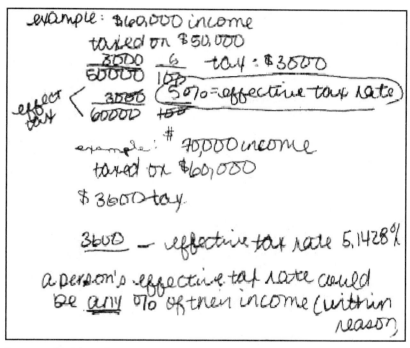

Source: NAEP Released Item 1992-12M12#9

Using the same principle of naming and noticing what the student did well and didn't do well, according to the criteria, feedback to this student might be something like the following. "You did your calculations accurately, and you explained your thinking in words. I could tell what you were thinking. You solved the first part of the problem by guessing and checking for the tax on a $60,000 income. That got you the right answer for part one, but it didn't help you solve part two. Let's work on how to model ideas in a word problem as an equation you can solve." Again, this is so much more informative to a student than to simply mark part one correct and part two incorrect. After that feedback, the teacher's next instructional move is also easy to decide: Provide this student a minilesson or some coaching on how to model word problems as equations.

These two examples, at two very different grade levels, illustrate how success criteria simplify deciding on what to say or write as feedback, which will save time, and focus the feedback on information students can use to travel the formative learning cycle, which will increase the effectiveness of your feedback. We think this is actually easier to see in the examples of students who need more help, such as Luther in the kindergarten example and the second student in the algebra example. Using the criteria illuminates that "next step" thinking for both students and teachers.

Some teachers in our PLCs wanted to give feedback on writing, spelling, and grammar on content-area assignments—for example, in social studies, science, and math. In elementary school, it is easy enough to justify doing this because written expression is a skill that crosses disciplines and is important for student thinking and learning. The PLC groups talked about the need to align feedback with learning goals and criteria. If written expression is taught along with the content, then it should be assessed. But if it is not part of what students are trying to learn, then it should take a back seat in your feedback.

In some cases, success criteria get conflated in teachers' minds, and they inadvertently give feedback on the wrong thing. For example, feedback on writing conventions can easily turn into one of those surface-level features that draw teachers' attention away from learning. As our PLC groups' discussions circled back to the success criteria for the assignments based on the standards and learning targets for that lesson, they found they did not always include targets about written expression. It was only through our reflective conversations that they realized they were trying to assess something—writing conventions—that they were not teaching.

Here is an example of an assessment with clear success criteria that the students did use. The teacher brought this example to the PLC to show her "aha" moment about the importance of both having clear criteria and using student self-assessment. From that perspective, it's a very successful example. The teacher's insight about how success criteria would help students move forward was a milestone for her, which makes this an example of teacher learning as well as student work.

A Classroom Example on Success Criteria: 4th Grade Science

Ms. Crispin was working on a science unit related to matter, properties, and change. She wanted the final product to be a foldable that showed what students had learned about the rock cycle and types of rocks, including meta-morphic, sedimentary, and igneous rocks. Her state standards (NCDPI, n.d.) were 4.P.2, "Understand the composition and properties of matter before and after they undergo a change or interaction" and 4.P2.3, "Classify rocks as metamorphic, sedimentary or igneous based on their composition, how they are formed and the processes that create them."

Unit goals included the following:

- Students have an understanding of the rock cycle.
- Students are able to label, describe, and provide facts about metamorphic, sedimentary, and igneous rocks.
- Students are able to define properties of rocks and minerals.

The assignment students were given was to "Create a foldable to show what I know about the rock cycle and types of rocks." The sample Ms. Crispin wanted to share with our group included one that helped her recognize the need for clear success criteria. Students had used books and the internet at school to gather information about rocks and minerals. In years past, Ms. Crispin had allowed students to read and go directly into the final draft of the foldable. This year, she decided she would allow them to write a rough draft and allow them to cross-check it against The Rock Cycle Project Rubric for Foldable, which she provided to students as their success criteria for learning as well as grading. Prior to grading the foldable this time, she conferenced with the students and allowed them to make changes to the final draft they submitted (see Figure 3.2).

Figure 3.2

The Rock Cycle Project Rubric for Foldable

Outside of Foldable
- Name and date on the top right front of foldable 5 ___
- Title: "The Rock Cycle" on the top middle 5 ___

Inside of Foldable (divided into two sections)
- Diagram of the rock cycle hand drawn with color 20 ___
- On the diagram the following must be labeled: 10 ___
  Melting, cooling and crystallizing, magma, heat and pressure. Rock broken down and carried away, the combinations of metamorphic rock, sedimentary rock, and igneous rock.

- Top left corner: Label "Igneous Rock" 10 ___
  Describe how igneous rock is formed and two additional facts about igneous rock (can be examples).

continued

Figure 3.2 (continued)

The Rock Cycle Project Rubric for Foldable

Inside of Foldable (divided into four sections)

- op left corner: Label "Igneous Rock" 10 ___

  Describe how igneous rock is formed and two additional facts about igneous rock (can be examples).

- Top right corner: Label "Sedimentary Rock" 10 ___

  Describe how sedimentary rock is formed and two additional facts about sedimentary rock (can be examples).

- Bottom left corner: Label "Metamorphic Rock" 10 ___

  Describe how metamorphic rock is formed and two additional facts about metamorphic rock (can be examples).

- Bottom right corner: Venn diagram 10 ___

  Tell how rocks and minerals are alike and different using a Venn diagram.

On the Back of the Foldable

- Name and define five properties of rocks and minerals 10 ___
- Overall presentation 10 ___

Make sure your foldable is neat, colorful, and legible.

One student, Jay, took this assignment sheet and used it like a checklist. Next to each of the bullets he put a large check mark. When the teacher looked at his work, she noticed his self-assessment had paid off: He had increased the level of detail for each type of rock.

Ms. Crispin reflected on what happened when she built in an opportunity for her students to use success criteria. She noted, "Doing a rough draft made me realize what the students need to work on instead of going right into the final draft. Even though this takes more time, it is important." She was able to use her assignment sheet as a tool for students to know and understand success criteria. This was new to her. When we talked about it, she realized she needed to explicitly teach them how to follow the self-assessment process, and she felt she could make her success criteria even more clear in future lessons. Allowing students to draft, cross-check against a rubric, then conference with her before submitting the final document is an example of utilizing the classroom formative assessment cycle. As a result of this process, she felt like she ended up with higher-quality work from students on this assignment.

As you can see, the assignment sheet mixes criteria about directions for the assignment with criteria that would be evidence of learning. For example, the quality of students' descriptions of how various types of rocks are formed

Student Work 3.5

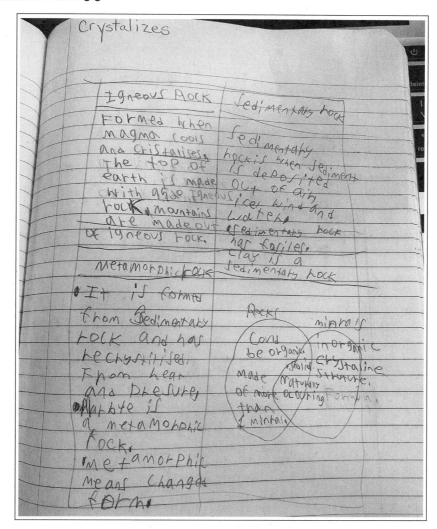

would be evidence of learning, at the Comprehension or Understand level in Bloom's terms, if students were able to put in their own words the facts and concepts they learned from their books and the internet. These are the criteria that Jay focused on, and the result was improved work. However, name, date, and title are aspects of the directions for the assignment. We suggested a next step for Ms. Crispin as she moves forward in developing expertise with success criteria would be to separate a directions checklist from the success criteria that gave evidence of learning. Students should still self-assess both, and she could give feedback on both, but the grading points should be based on the criteria that gave evidence of learning.

Characteristics of Effective Feedback

Effective feedback is an important component of the formative learning process (Brookhart, 2017). Clear learning goals (see Chapter 2) and effective feedback give students the information they need to aim for their learning targets and improve. As we have seen, the most effective feedback happens when the feedback is based on shared success criteria, when the students understand the criteria, and when those criteria are essential for the learning, not peripheral (e.g., about following directions or surface-level features of the work).

Feedback moves learning forward when students receive responses to their work from the teacher, themselves, or peers, and then have additional work opportunities in which they can use the feedback within the same formative learning cycle. Really effective feedback helps students get even clearer on where they are going, get a good sense of where they are now, and formulate a plan for what they will think or do next. Sometimes that planning includes setting new, small goals for themselves based on the success criteria. For example, a student might think, "I am going to add more details about the historical context into my report about the 1918 influenza epidemic."

We have used a metaphor of three lenses for looking at feedback as a way of describing how to give effective feedback that students can use in the formative learning cycle (Brookhart, 2017). The "micro view" calls to mind the lens in a microscope and reminds us to focus on the characteristics of the feedback message itself, whether written or oral. The "snapshot view" calls to mind taking a picture of learning at one moment in time. If you think of a feedback episode as a time when teachers look at student work, respond with a feedback message, and deliver the message to the student, and if you took a snapshot of that, would you see both the teacher and the student learning something? The teacher should learn something about how the student is thinking, and the student should learn something about his or her learning—where he or she is and where to go next. The "long view" calls to mind the lens in a telescope and reminds us the purpose of feedback is to move students closer to the learning goal. Does the teacher provide an opportunity for the students to use the feedback, instead of giving it to students with no chance of acting upon it? When the students use the feedback, do they in fact move closer to the learning goal?

You can use the three lenses to analyze the feedback you give your students. The Feedback Analysis Guide (see Figure 3.3) is a tool you can use to do that. If you think about it, you will see the guide does two things. First, the lenses ensure you connect the feedback to the formative learning cycle, because they move from the evidence of learning (the student work) through what you and the student learn from looking at it to the process and consequences of feedback use. Second, the questions in the guide are criteria for feedback. In the same way students use success criteria to learn, you can use these questions to learn to give more effective feedback.

First, let's take a moment to think about the micro lens. Feedback should describe student work in terms of the success criteria students have been using all along. It should come while students are still learning, so they have an opportunity to use it. It can focus on the work ("You used very evocative imagery in this poem") or the process students used to do the work ("You located a variety of different points of view about this issue, and that makes your essay stronger"), but it should not focus on the student personally. The tone of the message should be positive and supportive. Identify at least one way the student's work met the success criteria well and make at least one suggestion that would strengthen the work according to the criteria. Students will perceive this kind of constructive criticism as positive if they are not punished for it by receiving a poor grade and if they are given an opportunity to follow the suggestion and make their work better. Comments should be specific enough that students can follow through but not so specific the work is done for them, for example, by copyediting. And of course, comments should be clear to students, both physically—you might be surprised how often students report they cannot read their teachers' comments—and conceptually.

Next, think about the snapshot lens. This image is a good one for a book on looking at student work. Chapter 2 explored how looking at student work, or at least work from rich tasks, can give teachers a window into student thinking. Once you have such insights into student thinking, what can you do with them that will make the feedback episode a true episode of learning? One thing you can do is use these insights to craft your feedback: to select criteria for comment and to describe the students' work so they know where they are and where to go next. Another thing you can do is use these insights to target your next instructional moves to address not just any next steps, but the next steps that will best address students where they are and move

Figure 3.3
Feedback Analysis Guide

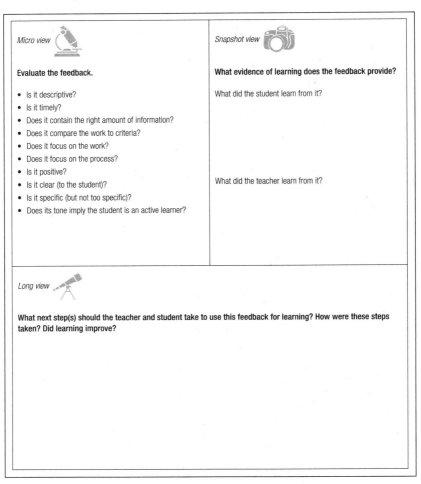

Micro view

Evaluate the feedback.

- Is it descriptive?
- Is it timely?
- Does it contain the right amount of information?
- Does it compare the work to criteria?
- Does it focus on the work?
- Does it focus on the process?
- Is it positive?
- Is it clear (to the student)?
- Is it specific (but not too specific)?
- Does its tone imply the student is an active learner?

Snapshot view

What evidence of learning does the feedback provide?

What did the student learn from it?

What did the teacher learn from it?

Long view

What next step(s) should the teacher and student take to use this feedback for learning? How were these steps taken? Did learning improve?

Source: From *How to Give Effective Feedback to Your Students, 2nd Edition* (p. 5), by S. M. Brookhart, 2017, Alexandria, VA: ASCD. Copyright 2017 by ASCD.

them along. The first of these moves, as the long view reminds us, should be to arrange for students to revise work or do additional practice.

Beesley and colleagues (2018) worked with middle school mathematics teachers in a program of professional development in formative assessment based in looking at student work. We'll say more about the format of that professional development in Chapter 5. For our discussion here, what is important to know is that the two biggest areas of improvement for the participating teachers were both about feedback. After learning about formative assessment by looking at student work, teachers' feedback moved from more evaluative to more descriptive—that is, from nonspecific judgment or praise to information about students' work relative to success criteria and suggestions for improvement. Also, teachers' feedback moved from lacking student involvement to encouraging students to reflect, identify where they need help, and revise their work or extend their learning.

Of course, the study results can't tell us why feedback was the biggest area for improvement, but we think the key lies in that snapshot view of feedback that emphasizes teachers should learn about student thinking when they look at student work. Having some insights into student thinking places the teacher—metaphorically, of course—inside the student's formative learning cycle. The obvious thing to do then would be to use those insights to craft feedback to help answer the questions "Where am I now?" and "Where to next?" The teachers Beesley and her colleagues worked with did that. The teachers we worked with did, too.

Teachers who are just beginning to look at student work as something more than grading papers may not have had much exposure to effective feedback practices. Moving from a traditional view like the one held by the supervising teacher in Chapter 1 to a view of feedback based in the formative learning cycle is a big shift and requires much conceptual work on the part of teachers. We noticed two misconceptions among the teachers we worked with. For both of these misconceptions, looking at student work served especially to strengthen their understanding and skills at feedback in similar ways to the teachers in Beesley's study: moving away from feedback as evaluation toward feedback as description and moving away from feedback as "fixing" the student's work toward feedback that the student could do something about.

If feedback is the teacher's evaluation of the student's work—that is, if feedback is just pronouncing judgment—then it doesn't matter much when the feedback comes. This was the first misconception about feedback we encountered in our work. Giving feedback in a timely way was a new idea for some people, "timely" here meaning not so much a number of hours or days but rather while the student is still working toward the learning goal. Looking at students' work and interpreting their thinking was a great entrée into the idea that feedback was best understood as help to the student rather than evaluation. Logically, then, the feedback needs to come while the student still needs the help. The teacher in the next example realized that as she looked at her students' social studies projects, and it was a major aha moment for her.

A Classroom Example on Feedback: 3rd Grade Social Studies

Ms. Edwards has been teaching about 10 years and currently teaches 3rd grade. During Black History Month, her grade level was planning a Wax Museum, a project fair to showcase students' projects about African American historical figures. Ms. Edwards was not the only audience for their work; other grade levels and any parents who had time to stop in during the regular school day were invited to this project fair.

Ms. Edwards invoked these state history standards:

> 3.H.1 Understand how events, individuals, and ideas have influenced the history of local and regional communities; 3.H.1.1 Explain key historical events that occurred in communities and regions over time; 3.H.1.2 Analyze the impact of contributions made by diverse historical figures in communities and regions over time; 3.H.1.3 Exemplify the ideas that were significant in the development of communities and regions. (NCDPI, n.d.)

Students were told they would be learning history by researching historical figures. The assignment directed them to choose and research a historical figure, create a tri-fold poster report, prepare a speech to present, and dress up as their historical figure. Students had an informational packet with directions, outlines, and a checklist for items that should be included. Finally, the students were expected to bring their costume to school for a dress rehearsal the day before the real Wax Museum and ultimately perform in the Wax Museum on a set date. The monthlong project was set up to include multiple checkpoints with different aspects of the projects, but it was primarily created as an out-of-school project.

Ms. Edwards did not share success criteria with her students beyond the directions checklist. However, when she met with us and shared the student work, her reflections were powerful and insightful. The first thing she noted after looking at the student projects was that some students clearly had significant parent help, while others worked more independently. Importantly, most of the parent help seemed to be for the purpose of making a professional-looking presentation, not increasing their children's understanding of historical figures. Here is an example that Ms. Edwards thought represented much parent assistance.

Student Work 3.6

It was not Ms. Edwards's intention to have parents help their children, but as the work came in, she increasingly worried that students might not actually understand the significance of the historical figure but only have a surface-level understanding. "I really should have set this project up differently. I am wondering if this project truly showed an understanding of history." As she talked with students at the dress rehearsal, she realized many of them could not answer questions about their figure. This outcome is related to the design of the assignment, which was a retelling task without criteria related to the learning goals. Telling this to Ms. Edwards would have been one thing, but seeing it happen in the student work in front of her made a powerful impression. Student Work 3.7 is an example of a project that Ms. Edwards thought represented a student's own work and is more what she had in mind. Notice that even this example, however, is basically a retelling of information.

As we continued to chat with Ms. Edwards, we talked about the need to have timely feedback that her students could use right away. She had been thinking about what was missing in the process and how she could increase student responsibility and learning in future projects. She noticed that she had not given feedback along the way, as students worked at home, but rather made assumptions about the work they were doing. Upon further consideration, she decided next time she could provide class time for students to do

Student Work 3.7

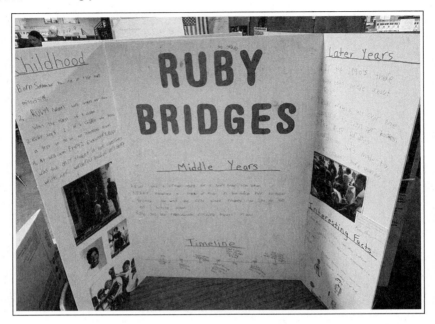

the research and create the boards in class so she could be more involved in the early stages of work and supply students with equal opportunities, instead of having parents as resources. Adding success criteria to the assignment from the beginning would have made this all possible.

In order to create avenues for more timely feedback, she decided it would be useful to create a couple of peer assessments a few times throughout the project as well as conference with students herself across the month. With this change, the at-home work could include prepping the costume and rehearsing. Ms. Edwards realized that shifting the way the work was done would give students more opportunities for feedback and also provide a way for them to use it.

Ms. Edwards's example illustrates a misconception about feedback timing, in this case with feedback arriving too late. The power in the example is not in the assignment, which was a basic retelling task that showcased students' (or parents'!) presentation skills more than their historical knowledge, but rather in the teacher's insights and the fact that they came directly from looking at student work.

The second misconception we found was that some of our PLC teachers had thought about feedback solely as criticism or as fixing the student's work. Their prior knowledge and experiences had made them think feedback is all about what students need to do differently. To notice and infer what thinking is on track according to criteria was a new idea for them. Looking at students' work helped bring home the point that feedback should be constructive, describing both strengths the work showed and weaknesses the student could do something about.

This realization helped with another issue, too. Many of the participants shared thoughts of feeling stuck and not being sure what feedback to give to the students or what to do next. The section on success criteria at the beginning of this chapter showed how the criteria supply language that can be used in feedback, so teachers are less likely to be stuck. In our PLCs, we found that role-playing giving feedback was also useful to "unstick" teachers who could not find the right words. Role-playing helped some teachers think of possible feedback and feel less stuck. We asked teachers who felt stuck to start with describing what the students did well in comparison to criteria. This helped open their minds so they could then move to constructive criticism, the "what next" part of the feedback. It was as if a gate opened. Many had been so hyperfocused on how to fix whatever it was that they were not noticing the "good stuff" in students' work, and once they could reference the good stuff against criteria, it was easier for them to generate feedback and then ultimately a possible next step.

The teacher in the following example was one of those who had reported feeling stuck, not knowing what to do. Her story shows that looking at student work with criteria in mind helped her unstick and move to feedback intended to help students make progress toward their learning target.

A Classroom Example on Feedback: Kindergarten English Language Arts

Ms. Rivers is a veteran teacher who has only recently come to teaching kindergarten. She loves working with this age group but sometimes finds herself unclear on how to move students with a wide range of achievement levels forward in their learning.

The lesson in question was a literature lesson based in state standard RL.K.3 (NCDPI, n.d.): "With prompting and support, identify characters, settings, and major events in a story." Today's learning target was "We are learning to identify characters and setting in a text." When we came together to examine her student work in a PLC session, Ms. Rivers said she felt stuck. She was not exactly sure what the work was telling her and wanted to be thoughtful about her feedback to her students.

She had read the book The Recess Queen *by Alexis O'Neill aloud to her students and then talked about characters, setting, and events in a story. In this book, the character Mean Jean starts off huge, and then at the end is the same size as everyone else. Ms. Rivers took time to point out that, in the book, the details in the pictures helped the readers understand even more about what the characters are like. She then released students to their desks to do an individual assignment: Draw characters and identify the setting in* The Recess Queen. *The success criteria were as follows: Students were to draw one or more characters with identifying details and draw some details of where the main events took place.*

When we examined the student work, we noticed students took up the idea of Mean Jean changing shape. If they drew an example from the book where she was doing something mean, they drew her bigger. If she was nice, they drew her the same size as other characters. Harold's drawing in Student Work 3.9 shows a clear example of this size differential.

We decided for this session, we would look at the standard and categorize the work into three different stacks: examples that needed some teacher support, like Harold's; examples that needed substantial support; and examples that needed no support. To Ms. Rivers's surprise, the majority of her students did not need support with this target. But she was still stuck. She had some students that did need support, and she didn't know what to tell them to do differently.

In this case, we decided not everyone needs to do it differently. Some students needed to keep doing what they were doing. We looked at the standard, looked at the students who did it with no teacher support, and decided to start there with possible feedback. For Pearl (see Student Work 3.8), it would sound something like this: "I can tell from your picture you can identify the main character and setting. That is exactly what we have been working on as a class. You have details like the soccer balls and goal that help me understand she is on the playground and that was part of the setting. Based on the details of your character, I can clearly identify who you drew. Continue to do this as we work on this target. This helps me see your thinking."

Looking at what went well created a clear focus and helped Ms. Rivers feel less stuck. Starting with what students did well in comparison to the clear success criteria helped her move to possible feedback not just for Pearl but for all students who fell into this category.

Student Work 3.8

For students like Harold (see Student Work 3.9), the feedback needed to be different. He needed some support in order to clearly identify the characters and setting. He had two characters on his paper—one very large figure representing Mean Jean and a smaller figure—but the setting was unclear.

We went through the same process to think about feedback that would be useful for him and for other students in this category. What did he do well, and what were some suggestions for improvement? We referenced the success criteria and came up with "Harold, tell me about your picture. Oh, OK, I see you drew Mean Jean bigger than Katie Sue. That tells me you know two characters. What can you tell me about the setting? Do you remember anything about where this story took place? OK . . . then can you add those details to your picture?"

Ms. Rivers found she had very few students in the final category in the sorting, work showing students who needed the most teacher support. For students like Jason (see Student Work 3.10), her feedback had to be extra

Student Work 3.9

specific. He had drawn a large head on the paper, and it lacked details or descriptive markers.

For Jason and the other two students in this category, Ms. Rivers needed to gather more thinking from her students. The feedback went something like "Jason, I can tell you were trying to draw a person from the book. Can you tell me about it? Oh, that's Mean Jean? OK. What else do you remember about her? Oh, do you think you could add some of those ideas to your picture? That way I know you were trying to draw her and not Katie Sue." Feedback dialogues with students are a great way to help clarify what students were thinking.

At the end of the PLC session, Ms. Rivers realized her feeling of being stuck had come from anxiety over what feedback to give the students who needed substantial support, fears that were allayed once she realized how to use the language of the success criteria to frame her feedback. She also real-ized that her fears about those few students were overwhelming her thoughts about this lesson: "I realized that these are the students I was focused on, but the majority of my class is on track. I really don't need to spend a lot of time on this standard without adding on to it. If I don't go ahead and go beyond the standard, the majority of my class won't continue to grow with this."

At the end of our conversation, there was a lot of student learning to celebrate. Instead of being focused on how to fix whatever she thought was

Student Work 3.10

wrong, Ms. Rivers started to notice all the things her students could already do. She had realized that what was making her uncomfortable was thinking that feedback was a criticism of the student, and when she learned otherwise, her problem was solved.

This example shows a teacher who shifted her focus from thinking of feedback as addressing what students did wrong to thinking of feedback in terms of where students were going. This was an important reorientation. She moved from a reactive view of feedback to a proactive view, based in moving students along the formative learning cycle. She discovered that she need only describe evidence of student learning against criteria aligned with standards. If the criteria are in place, many of the words are already there. This made it easier for her to generate specific feedback to keep all students' learning moving forward, and it helped her feel less at a loss about this important aspect of her work.

The Role of Students in Feedback

This book is about teachers looking at student work and how it advances their understanding of student thinking, the quality of their feedback, their ability to select appropriate next instructional moves, and their growth as professionals. Therefore, this chapter has focused on teacher learning about feedback. You will have noticed, however, that the stories we shared about our work with teachers involved students as well. Before we move on to next instructional moves, we think the role of students in feedback is worth mentioning.

Students need to understand their feedback and have the emotional strength to respond. Research on how that happens is ongoing in both K–12 (Leighton, 2019) and university (Winstone, Nash, Parker, & Rowntree, 2017) contexts. How students perceive and receive feedback—and different students receive feedback differently—is an important part of the process about which teachers should be informed and to which teachers should be sensitive.

Leighton (2019) describes how the classroom social environment, including teacher and peer relations, may or may not support trust between students and teachers. The classroom environment affects the degree to which feedback can be formative. If students do not feel safe asking for help, many students will not do it. Students' understanding of the nature of learning, of what it means to learn, is shaped by teachers' words and actions as well. Some classrooms foster an understanding of mistakes as opportunities to learn and intelligence as something that can be learned. Other classrooms foster an understanding of mistakes as evidence of being "dumb." In classrooms with safe learning environments and where students see learning in terms of goals they can reach if they apply themselves, Leighton (2019) proposes, teachers' feedback on student work can be formative. In classrooms low on trust and empathy, where learning is seen as something some students naturally do better than others, teachers' feedback on student work is likely to be "feckless" (p. 35). We looked up the word, just to make sure we were remembering correctly: *feckless* means ineffective or irresponsible. And that does just about sum it up! No matter how lovely your feedback is in terms of the micro view of the message, if students are too embarrassed or afraid to hear it, or do not think it matters, your feedback will not be effective.

One teacher we worked with seemed to know this intuitively. She said she got frustrated with writing feedback on students' papers because she did not think they would actually read it. Alice suggested she test out a way to make the communication two-way: Let students know that feedback is important and useful to all parties to learning, student and teacher alike, and allow them space to write back in some way. The teacher liked the idea and said she would give it a try.

Winstone and colleagues (2017) focused on the understandings and emotions students need in order to actively receive, engage with, and use feedback. They looked at studies done in the university setting, although some K–12 educators are interested in this work as well. They proposed four "recipience processes" (p. 17) students need to bring to the table in order to benefit from the feedback they receive. They named their taxonomy of these processes students can use to benefit from feedback SAGE: Self-appraisal, Assessment literacy, Goal-setting and self-regulation, and Engagement and motivation. Students who judge that they can be active learners, who understand the relation between assessment and learning and the role of criteria, who can explicitly articulate what they want to achieve and work toward it, and who are enthusiastic and open to receiving information about their performance will be more likely to engage with and use the feedback they receive.

In the example below, looking at student work helped Ms. Trent notice that student engagement and self-regulation decreased because of ineffective feedback. In this case, the teacher established appropriate criteria and gave substantive feedback that could have been effective. But the feedback was oral and thus dependent on students' memories. Lessons came only once or twice a week, so the opportunity to apply the feedback came days after it was given and, in many cases, forgotten. These conditions did not allow students to engage with and use the feedback they received. Looking at her students' work helped the teacher realize that they had not been able to take up and apply their feedback, which led to her decision to redesign her feedback in the future.

A Classroom Example on Feedback: 3rd Grade Science Enrichment

Ms. Trent is a seasoned educator with a variety of experiences in schools who is currently the schoolwide enrichment teacher. Her enrichment classes are designed as a support and extension for the regular learning in grade K–5 classrooms, focused on developing students' creativity and problem-solving skills. In her teaching, she uses many student-led projects aimed at authentic audiences.

As part of a unit on ecosystems, students were studying plants. The learning goals came from state standards (NCDPI, n.d.): 3.L.2, "Understand

*how plants survive in their environments"; 3.L.2.1, "Remember the function of
the following structures as it relates to the survival of plants in their environments: Roots – absorb nutrients; Stems – provide support; Leaves – synthesize
food; Flowers – attract pollinators and produce seeds for reproduction";
3.L.2.2, "Explain how environmental conditions determine how well plants
survive and grow"; 3.L.2.3, "Summarize the distinct stages of the life cycle
of seed plants"; and 3.L.2.4, "Explain how the basic properties (texture and
capacity to hold water) and components (sand, clay and humus) of soil determine the ability of soil to support the growth and survival of many plants."*

*Ms. Trent summarized the learning target for one part of the project as "We
are learning to understand how plants survive in their environments." Students
planted two plants and kept a log of what they noticed about their plants over
time in observation logs. She gave the students these success criteria:*

- *Notice and note detailed changes from week to week in the log.*
- *Use relevant science vocabulary.*
- *Make connections and applications with the regular classroom science
content.*

*Students had four days to observe. Because Ms. Trent is a schoolwide
enrichment teacher, she does not see her students every day. She typically
sees them once or twice a week, depending on how the rotation is working. In
this case, this allowed for plant growth to happen in between observations.*

*Ms. Trent envisioned this log as a way for students to track their thinking
and use it for oral discussions in class. Her hope was that the students would
increase their understanding of how plants survive in their environments over
the weeks of observations. While students made observations, Ms. Trent circu-
lated around the room to make comments and offer on-the-spot oral feedback
to students.*

*It was not until later that Ms. Trent took a deep dive into the observa-
tion logs. Looking at this student work brought several insights. She noticed
Everett was able to observe which seeds were germinating, and he drew some
sketches of germinating seeds. However, except for one other detail for Plant B
on Day 1, where he added that the soil was damp, what looked like a full observation log was really just a list of which seeds had germinated. There was no
description of plant structures or growing conditions. Ms. Trent felt like she
really needed to push Everett to write in more detail so he could clearly follow
the changes from week to week.*

Student Work 3.11

Looking across the observation logs for the class, Ms. Trent noticed a pattern. Many students started off strong and then dropped off over the following observations. As time passed, they used fewer science vocabulary words and noted fewer details. She felt they expressed less ownership of the work and poorer application of concepts.

Upon reflection, Ms. Trent decided that the next time she did a similar project, she needed to increase her feedback in some way along the way and throughout the course of the observations. She said, "I am not sure they can actually hold onto my feedback without me (or them) writing it down. I need to figure out a way to seize on some thinking in the moment because it is so valuable. Just doing oral feedback is not working overall." Taking it one step further, she said, "I realize that some of the pieces didn't come together as I *had hoped. Without giving written feedback weekly, it did not work as I had planned. The student ownership and grasp of the concepts ended up being spotty."*

While we realize, with Ms. Trent, that her feedback did not have the effect she intended, she deserves great credit for the depth and quality of her reflections. She will ultimately be more effective with feedback because of looking at her students' work deeply, reflecting on what they needed, and making plans for providing it to them.

Summary

Effective feedback describes student work against criteria. It helps students see where they are in their pursuit of a learning target and where they need to go next. This is most likely to happen if the feedback message has the characteristics listed in the feedback analysis guide in Figure 3.3, if teachers as well as students learn something from the feedback episode, and if students have opportunities to use the feedback—the main thing missing in the story of Ms. Trent's plant observation logs. Looking at student work is a powerful way for teachers to learn these skills. At the same time, students must have both the understanding and emotional readiness to take up their feedback and act on it. Students who have regular practice with criteria, descriptive feedback, opportunities to use feedback, and reflection time can grow these qualities.

Coach's Corner: Hints for Helping Teachers Learn to Provide Effective Feedback

- Role-playing giving student feedback is extremely helpful for participants. Role-playing can be especially effective for teachers who are anxious about discussing feedback with colleagues.
- It is important to have participants deliberately practice looking at student work for what the students did well. This is a good antidote to the conventional wisdom that feedback means corrections or fixes and helps develop feedback skills. It also may help diffuse the emotions some teachers feel looking at their students' work in a group setting.

- Feedback is not about what is wrong with student work. Help teachers keep top-of-mind that it is about where students are going with their learning. The formative learning cycle is a simple way to think of this.

- For teachers who are already developing the knowledge and skills required for giving useful feedback, a deeper dive into success criteria is helpful if time allows.

 Reflection Questions

1. Locate or think about some feedback you have given on student work that was particularly effective, in your view. How do you know it was effective? How did it exhibit some of the characteristics of effective feedback described in this chapter?

2. Why do you think it is so important to describe strengths as well as areas for improvement in student work? Can you connect your reasoning to the characteristics of effective feedback and/or conditions for student receptivity to feedback discussed in this chapter?

4

Deciding on Next Instructional Moves

Decisions about next instructional moves are more effective when they are based on an understanding of student thinking than when they are based solely on the correctness of work. Evaluations of correctness alone lead to next instructional moves like reviewing what was already taught, often in the same way it had already been taught, and providing additional practice opportunities at the same general kind of work that was not correct in the first place. When teachers understand how students are thinking about a concept, they can diagnose next learning needs more precisely, target next instructional moves to focus on specific misunderstandings or naïve under-standings, and assign further work aimed at these specific needs.

Documented Difficulty of Making Instructional Decisions from Formative Assessment

Research evidence and our experience with teachers both suggest that mak-ing instructional decisions from formative assessment information has been more difficult for teachers than interpreting student thinking. Research has found that the most difficult aspect of formative assessment for teachers lies in using the information appropriately (Heritage et al., 2009; Schneider & Gowan, 2013).

Heritage and colleagues (2009) presented 118 6th grade teachers with a series of performance tasks in which teachers were asked to review student work. The student work they looked at was student responses to mathematics problems assessing key principles required for mastery of Algebra I: the distributive property, solving equations, and rational number equivalence. After reviewing each student response, teachers were asked the following (p. 25):

1. What is the key principle that these assessments address? Why do students need to understand this principle for Algebra I?

2. What inferences would you draw from this student's responses? What does this student know? What does this student not know?

3. If you were this child's teacher, what written feedback would you give to this student?

4. If this student were in your class, based on your responses to questions 2 and 3, what would you do next in your instruction?

As you can see, question 1 asks about content knowledge, question 2 asks about inferring student thinking, question 3 asks about feedback, and question 4 asks about next instructional moves. A group of university mathematics experts and expert teachers categorized teacher responses into a scoring rubric. A method called a generalizability study was used to figure out how much of the variability in teachers' scores was related to teacher, rater, mathematics principle (whether the student work was about the distributive property, solving equations, or rational number equivalence), and type of task (identifying the key principle, evaluating student thinking, or planning the next instructional step). Notice that feedback was not included in type of task; there was some missing data for question 3. The results suggested that type of task made the greatest difference in teachers' scores, and that no matter what the mathematics principle, determining the next instructional step was more difficult for teachers than identifying the key principle or evaluating student thinking. The authors suggested that the reasons might be related to teachers' needing more understanding of learning progressions, more knowledge for teaching mathematics (pedagogical content knowledge), and deeper mathematics knowledge. In any case, the clear finding that deciding on next instructional moves is more difficult for teachers than other tasks was a big discovery.

Schneider and Gowan (2013) worked with 23 upper-elementary mathematics teachers. Teachers looked at five pieces of student work, each one a student answer to a constructed-response mathematics question. Teachers looked at each item first without the student response, then looked at the student work, and finally answered four questions (p. 195):

1. What does this item measure?

2. Based upon the student's response, what can you infer that this student knows? What does the student not yet know?

3. Provide specific feedback to this student about what he or she should do next as if you are writing on the student's work.

4. If this were your student, what would you do next instructionally?

As you can see, the questions paralleled the Heritage and colleagues (2009) study, asking about content knowledge, inferring student thinking, feedback, and next instructional moves. Schneider and Gowan were able to include all four questions in their analyses, and they found that for these 23 math teachers, feedback was consistently the more difficult task for teachers, more so than analyzing student understanding or next instructional steps.

Of course, we can't conclude from these two studies whether giving effective feedback is more difficult than deciding on next instructional moves, or vice versa, in general. However, there is enough evidence here to conclude that both of these tasks are difficult for teachers. There are many potential reasons why this may be the case, including teachers' perceptions of the assessments and resulting information, time and scheduling constraints, and, most notably, the tendency of teachers to look at the quantity of learning (e.g., number correct) instead of the quality of learning (i.e., what students are thinking) (Ruiz-Primo & Li, 2013). Improving your skill at taking the important step from evidence to instructional decision making is possibly the most compelling reason to change how you look at student work.

Both studies we just described had teachers look at student work in their content area but from students who were not their own. What happens when teachers look at their own students' work? Ruiz-Primo, Kroog, and Sands (2015) studied how mathematics and science teachers responded after looking at student work during lessons in their own classrooms. They explored what types of instructional moves teachers made, using videos from their teaching. About three-quarters of the time, after observing students' work in either mathematics or science lessons, teachers either made general statements to the whole class or did not make any content-based responses to the work. In much smaller proportions, teachers sometimes followed observation of student work by solving problems with students, solving problems without students (e.g., by demonstrating), reclarifying the task, providing the correct answer, or reteaching. These percentages are averages across videos of the formative assessment practices of 20 teachers, and individual teachers did differ in the percentage of response types in their classes. But these averages paint a picture that illustrates feedback and next instructional moves are difficult for teachers, even in their own classrooms. Much of the time, after observing students doing a task, it seems that teachers may just make general statements to the whole class or not respond at all to the student work. In other words, they forfeit an opportunity to target feedback and next instructional moves that will be formative for students.

For us, this research on the difficulty of feedback and next instructional moves is a siren call to engage teachers in looking at student work. As the examples we have shown so far demonstrate, looking at student work thoughtfully can help teachers develop these important skills. Student work done in the classroom is, at least most of the time, a fabulous source of information for next instructional moves because it is close to the learning. It is close in time and space, arising in the classroom context during the sequence of lessons when students are learning something. It is the closest match to teachers' and students' informational and diagnostic needs because the questions and tasks to which students respond are typically at the lesson or unit goal level; that is, the information is more fine-grained and detailed than large-scale measures of a whole standard. And, as our work with teachers showed us, looking at the work of their own students is interesting to teachers. It is relevant to their own instruction and to students they know and care about. This is the space in which most teachers "live" professionally.

Targeting Next Instructional Moves to Student Thinking

Teachers who look at student work for correctness mostly focus on reteaching in areas of weakness—areas in which many students scored low. This strategy relies on the unsound logic of doing the same thing as before and expecting a different result. However, when teachers look at student work for evidence of student thinking, they get clues about students' misconceptions or misunderstandings as well as clues about what students already do under-stand. Next instructional moves can be targeted more precisely at areas of weakness and can sometimes leverage areas of strength to do so.

Giving effective feedback (see Chapter 3) can be the beginning of a next instructional move if it is coupled with planning opportunities for students to use the feedback to revise their work as part of subsequent instruction. Beyond that, teachers' instructional moves can cover a range that moves from less to more of a learning-goal orientation and from less to more sup-port of student self-regulation of learning.

Ruiz-Primo and Brookhart (2018) described a continuum of potential next instructional moves that goes from evaluative to descriptive, a dimen-sion we showed in Chapter 3 was of central importance to feedback as well. Just as descriptive feedback is more formative than evaluative feedback, next instructional moves that are descriptive and show students how they can move forward are more formative than evaluative statements about what students can and cannot do. The continuum also moves from no student participation through student co-participation in the instruction. The more description and the more student participation in a teacher's next instruc-tional move, the more formative that next move can be. Conversely, next instructional moves that are evaluative and do not allow student participa-tion inhibit students' progress on the formative learning cycle. Ruiz-Primo and Brookhart (2018, p. 67) describe next instructional moves this way, in order from least formative to most formative.

LEAST FORMATIVE

- Provide correct answer with no explanation. (Evaluative, no student participation)
- Make physical changes in the classroom or temporal shifts in the dis-cussion of topics without explanations to the students. Reclarify the task. (Descriptive, no student participation)
- Model/review how to solve the problem/task without the help of the student. Provide correct answer with an explanation. (Descriptive, no student participation)
- Solve the problem/task with the help of the student(s). Help to reinforce the strategies used in that type of problem/task. (Descriptive, student participation)

- Co-construct with student(s) the bigger idea or the strategy that is the focus of a type of problem, something that goes beyond the task at hand. (Descriptive, student participation)

MOST FORMATIVE

This continuum was devised from Ruiz-Primo and her colleagues' research with mathematics and science teachers, so it is focused on next instructional moves common in those disciplines. We generalized the continuum to include potential next instructional moves for a wider range of subject areas. This should help you envision what kinds of instructional responses could follow from looking at student work. Figure 4.1 describes next instructional moves in order from least to most formative, in the sense of moving students along on the formative learning cycle.

We do not mean to imply that Figure 4.1 moves from "bad" to "good." There are times when simply going over an assignment (evaluative, no student participation) is all you have time for. Most of the time, however, you will want to make the most formative next instructional move possible given your context. We suggest that evaluative and nonformative next instructional moves happen more often than necessary and hope that the continuum in Figure 4.1 makes you more aware of options for next instructional moves.

Another thing to note about the continuum is that the less formative end of the continuum does not require you to glean any more information from student work than you would get from the grading papers orientation. Simply knowing whether student work was correct or incorrect would support the less formative next instructional moves on the left of the figure. As you move toward the right side of the continuum, you see more formative next instructional moves. Notice that the options on the right side do require that you have looked at student work for evidence of student thinking. Simple knowledge of correctness is not detailed and descriptive enough to support more formative decisions about next instructional moves—for example, mini-lessons, revisions of work, differentiation and student choice, and so on.

The column labeled "Evaluative, No Student Participation" describes teaching based on a grading papers approach to student work. One option is reviewing the assignment or assessment. Most students will perceive this as an exercise in summative thinking carried out so they can see what they got wrong. Another option is going on with lessons as planned even though the student work suggests some students are not ready. Distinguish this

Figure 4.1

Possible Next Instructional Moves, from Least to Most Formative

Evaluative, No Student Participation	Descriptive, No Student Participation	Descriptive, Minimal Student Participation	Descriptive, Student Participation	Descriptive, Students Co-Construct Meaning
• Go over the assignment with students, providing correct answers. • Go on with instruction as planned even though some students are not ready.	• Describe the task again. Go on with instruction as planned after this brief reclarification.	• Show students how to do the work, either by modeling or by reviewing an example. • Show additional examples. • Repeat elements of the previous lesson in the same manner as taught the first time. • Assign additional reading or viewing.	• Have students help demonstrate how to solve the problem. • Facilitate a short class discussion about the concept, issue, or task. • Present a minilesson focused on specific areas of need. • Have students revise their work (if the task is open-ended) or do additional practice questions (if the questions are right/wrong) according to the feedback they received. • Reteach the lesson (or part of it) with different materials and activities than before. Build background knowledge if needed. • Present opportunities for students to apply ideas with active learning methods (which differ by subject area).	• Deconstruct the task or assignment with students, helping them see how what they are learning in this task connects with prior learning and with intended future learning. • Have students revise their work (if the task is open-ended) or do additional practice questions (if the questions are right/wrong) according to the feedback they received and reflect on what they learned by doing that. • Differentiate the next lesson, taking into account the variety of student starting points. • Offer students opportunities to choose an alternate way to show their thinking (e.g., create a speech, research a topic of interest, do an inquiry project).

Least Formative ←   → **Most Formative**

from going on with a lesson as planned when the work shows students are ready for it (recall Ms. Rivers's example in Chapter 3), which is a formative instructional move.

The column labeled "Descriptive, No Student Participation" describes a minimal change in instruction based on students' work. Clarifying the task again may help some students get clearer on the learning goal they are aiming for. In the case of Ms. Trent's example in Chapter 3, this might mean saying something like "Remember, boys and girls, we were looking for a description of what the seedlings looked like, not just a note about whether they had germinated." The shift from an evaluative to a descriptive instructional stance is helpful, but so much more could be done.

The column labeled "Descriptive, Minimal Student Participation" moves toward the formative because students are brought into the learning process. For example, Ms. Trent could have demonstrated for students how to write a detailed observation of the plantings. They would then have a model to follow. Next, she might have them redo their own plant observations.

The column labeled "Descriptive, Student Participation" shows next instructional moves that make students a more active part of the learning. For example, Ms. Trent could have students look at examples of classmates' plant observations and make suggestions, based on criteria or models, and have students revise their work.

The column labeled "Descriptive, Students Co-Construct Meaning" shows next instructional moves that make students active not only in the learning but in conceptualizing what is to be learned. For example, Ms. Trent could have students look at examples of classmates' plant observations and make suggestions based on criteria or models, have students revise their work, and then have them discuss how much more they could learn about seed germination from their revised observation logs. She might then have some students who were still having trouble with the process of scientific observation document the seedlings' growth by creating a photo log and supplying written descriptions with the photos, while others who had shown facility with scientific observation might plan and implement an experiment comparing different soil and water combinations, where they would use their observational skills and also explore other aspects of the plants standard.

We can illustrate the range of options for next instructional moves by considering some anonymous student work. Suppose a high school science teacher is working on the Next Generation Science Standards' Science and

Engineering Practice Standard of planning and carrying out investigations in the Disciplinary Core Idea of earth materials and systems. Students are learning about experimental design, including concepts like independent, dependent, and control variables. The teacher asks students to write a response to the following prompt. She specifies the answer should have two parts: equipment and procedure.

> Oil is spilled onto the water from an oceangoing tanker. Investigators want to know whether wave motion will help disperse the oil. Design an experiment that they can carry out in a laboratory to find out whether wave motion will help disperse the oil. Describe the equipment they should use and the procedure they should follow. (NAEP Released Item 2005-12S13#11)

One student answers with a minimal, but complete, answer:

Student Work 4.1

2 large pools of water, oil, wave maker
1. Fill the pools with water.
2. Put the "spilled" oil in both pools.
3. Make artificial waves in one pool.
4. See if the waves helped to disperse the oil.

However, the teacher notices quite a few partially correct answers like the following two. They each differ slightly in quality, but all share the same main issue of lacking a control.

Student Work 4.2

wave machine, fish tank, vegetable oil
Create an "oilslick" in the fishtank, and set the wave machine up in the tank, creating waves. Make observations as to whether the slick breaks up and disperses throughout the tank, or remains together.

Student Work 4.3

large bowl, water, oil (cooking oil or black oil)
In a large bowl filled with water pour some of the oil in one area (enough so it can spread). Then with a gentle rocking motion, move the bowl to see if the oil disperses.

The teacher looks over the work from this and other questions done in class. She might simply mark them as correct or incorrect, or she might look for evidence of student thinking. If she looked for student thinking, she would find the most salient aspect was that many students were able to identify appropriate materials for an investigation and describe a procedure but did not have a control. For example, the first student built a simple control variable into the investigation by comparing oil dispersion in a pool with waves to the dispersion in a pool without waves. The second and third students, and others like them, did not have such a comparison, which left the investigation with no way to evaluate the effectiveness of the waves in dispersing the oil.

Using the continuum of next instructional moves from less to more formative in Figure 4.1 helps us identify a range of potential next instructional moves for this teacher in Figure 4.2.

Any one of these approaches may be appropriate in some situations, but we hope you can see that the more formative next instructional moves, and those tied more closely to the evidence of student thinking, are more likely to support student learning. These are the kinds of next instructional moves we encourage you to use whenever possible.

We also hope that this thought experiment about the range of next instructional moves after looking at student work gives you a paradigm you can use to envision the next instructional moves you might take in your own teaching, whatever the content area or grade level. Finally, we want to reemphasize the point that looking at student work was what made any of these choices possible.

Learning About Next Instructional Moves by Looking at Student Work

We illustrate the importance of being as formative as possible in selecting next instructional moves after looking at student work by showing how teachers in our PLCs grew in this understanding. In fact, once teachers have begun to think of student work as a source of information about student thinking, they are almost compelled to use this information. Who would stop at understanding inside their own heads what students are thinking and not take the next logical step of trying to help them continue to learn?

One of the things we learned is that the analysis of pedagogy in addition to student thinking became more evident as the PLC work went on. At the beginning, looking at student work to interpret student thinking was new

Figure 4.2
Possible Next Instructional Moves for the
Experimental Design Example

Evaluative, No Student Participation

The teacher could pass back the questions, marked with a check or X, and then go on to the next lesson.

Descriptive, No Student Participation

The teacher could go over the question, telling students this question was about carrying out investigations and that what she was looking for was evidence of independent, dependent, and control variables. She might say something like "Many of you designed investigations that did not have a control." She might assume that explanation was sufficient for students to understand where they went wrong and go on to the next lesson.

Descriptive, Minimal Student Participation

The teacher might show a complete example, perhaps the first student's work shown above, and explain why it was complete. Then she might repeat a portion of her lecture on control variables or show a video about experimental control.

Descriptive, Student Participation

The teacher might ask students, "What do you think a good answer to this question should look like?" Then, using brainstorming techniques, she would help the class come up with an acceptable answer. In the process, she would help students articulate the concept of experimental control. She could then give back the students' work and have them work in pairs to create a strong answer to the question.

Descriptive, Students Co-Construct Meaning

The teacher might ask students, "What do you think a good answer to this question should look like?" Then, using brainstorming techniques, she would help the class come up with an acceptable answer. In the process, she would help students articulate the concept of experimental control. Then, she might ask the students, "Why do you think it's important to build controls into experiments?" The discussion could range beyond an experiment about waves dispersing oil to more general concepts in planning and carrying out investigations. She could then give back the students' work and have them self-assess using criteria about experimental design. Some students would find their work in need of revision and would be allowed do that. Other students might find that they had hit all the criteria (independent, dependent, and control variables, etc.) and would answer another, slightly more difficult, question about investigation in earth materials and systems.

enough to some teachers that they focused solely on the interpretation. But this evolved into sharing ideas for the next instructional move that included pedagogy and not just content. Several teachers, without prompting, started to analyze not just the student and content but also their pedagogy in their comments and reflections.

Focusing on student thinking rather than correctness led teachers from several grade levels and content areas in our PLC work to an interesting insight about some whom they had considered their "top" students. They noticed some of these students were not able to share their thinking in a way that met their learning targets and success criteria. This led to a deep discussion about the difference between students' surface-level comprehension of content and their abilities to articulate their thinking processes by writing or drawing. This is evident in the 3rd grade science enrichment example in Chapter 3, in the 4th grade math example below, and in the 1st grade math example later in this chapter.

A Classroom Example on Next Instructional Moves: 4th Grade Math

Ms. Jacobs had been working on fractions with her 4th graders. Fractions can be difficult for students, and in this lesson, students were expected to extend their understanding of what they already know about fractions. Ms. Jacobs was teaching state standard (NCDPI, n.d.) 4.NF.A.2: "Compare two fractions with different numerators and different denominators." She shared this learning target for today's lesson: "We are learning to use our understanding of comparing fractions to solve word problems."

Each table group had a word problem to solve involving fractions. Students were required to write explanations to show the strategy they used and how they solved the problems. Students worked collaboratively but had to record their thinking as individuals. The teacher shared these success criteria, to which students referred as they worked:

- *I can identify key words to solve word problems.*
- *I can use strategies to compare two fractions.*
- *I can correctly solve word problems involving fractions.*
- *I can explain my thinking when comparing fractions using precise math language.*

Ms. Jacobs created the small table groups, and each table had a different word problem comparing fractions. The students within the group were differentiated based on their prior performances with fractions. Students were able to choose which strategy they wanted to use to solve the problem: model, fraction bar, or butterfly. Ms. Jacobs had also taught her students to use a graphic organizer that she called the KFC to help students show what they Know, what they need to Find Out, and to Come up with a solution.

Ms. Jacobs gave problems with 3 fractions, as in the work sample below, to groups with students she considered to be solid in their understanding. This problem read, "David completed 1/3 of his homework. Shawn completed 2/5 of his homework, and Raymond completed 3/4 of his homework. Which boy completed the most homework? Discuss how you found your answer with your group. Then write to explain your thinking."

Student Work 4.4

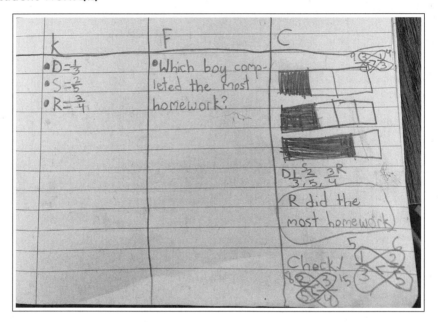

When she looked at the work, she noticed this student had no problems with the graphic organizer part of this lesson. The student put down the initials for the names in the problem (D= David, R= Raymond, etc.) and accurately wrote the corresponding fractions. She took time to identify key words and clearly identified what she needed to find out in the F column. She was able to utilize three different strategies for solving the problem (model, fraction, and butterfly). Because Ms. Jacobs was walking around and listening in as students worked, she was able to verify that all the group members had participated in the discussion. She said, "The team discussed these models as a group and each individual wrote it in their math journal."

In this case, the student thinking displayed in the sample showed Ms. Jacobs that the student knew the concepts and understood how to compare fractions, how to use multiple strategies, and how to check answers successfully. The area of need emerged when she looked at the constructed response.

The problem had asked students to "write to explain your thinking," and she had wanted more specific mathematical language and discourse included in the explanation. She decided to give feedback to this student that included expanding her ideas to include more math language and also articulating what she knew about math. Ms. Jacobs pointed out that this is one of her highest-achieving math students but she "still has room to grow."

For her next instructional moves, Ms. Jacobs recognized she needed to make some adjustments. The next time they did a lesson including written responses, she would need to build in additional time to help students get familiar with the criteria for complete explanations. Students need time to write, use feedback from Ms. Jacobs, and then add to their writing. "Even if they don't have a chance to correct their thinking on paper, I could allow them to share with a partner how to include more math language in their responses."

One of the reasons that this professional development was fun for teachers was that looking at their own students' work and linking it to their own instruction struck many of them as an inherently fascinating process. One 1st grade teacher said, "I enjoy thinking about where students are and what comes next—how I can identify the zone of proximal development but also hold students accountable for articulating their thinking." Here is an example of her thinking.

A Classroom Example on Next Instructional Moves: 1st Grade Math

Ms. Forrester was teaching math for state standards (NCDPI, n.d.) 1.NBT.2, "Understand two digits represented by 10s and 1s," and 1.NBT. 4, "Add within 100 using concrete materials, drawings, and strategies based on place value explaining the reasoning used." In today's lesson, Ms. Forrester shared that students were aiming for three learning targets:

- *I can break apart numbers that make sense to my brain.*
- *I can represent those numbers by drawing or writing.*
- *I can show my thinking about math.*

The task involved estimating numbers and explaining their reasoning using a variety of materials, drawings, and strategies. In this assignment, students were given Skittles and had to justify the number of Skittles that would fit in a light bulb, then record their thinking in their journals.

When Ms. Forrester examined the journals, Ren's work surprised her. She said, "This student's thinking is very high-level. But the underpinning is not what I expected."

Student Work 4.5

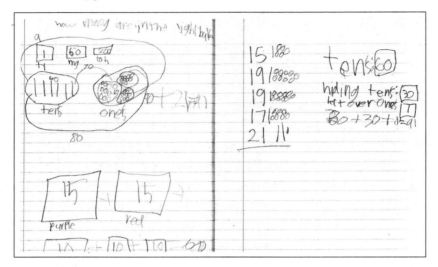

She noticed he was able to estimate and showed equations with multiple addends. She also noticed his answer was informed by breaking numbers apart—it showed decomposition of numbers into 10s and 1s to combine like units. However, estimating is just the beginning of working with place value. Upon further analysis, Ms. Forrester was able to see that Ren could decompose, organize, make 10s, count by 10s, and show models.

She decided that her feedback needed to help guide Ren toward abstract reasoning. As part of the methodology of moving students from concrete to representational to abstract reasoning in math, Ms. Forester wanted to push a little to see if she could scaffold Ren's thinking toward the abstract. Focusing on justification would help her see if he had the language and capability to work in the abstract form. Her feedback ended up sounding something like this: "I see you have made a clear drawing of 10s and 1s. Is it possible to do this without drawing 10s and 1s? Could you use a number representation here? How could you show that?" Then she gave Ren an opportunity to think about how he could show that in another way. For her next instructional move, she asked Ren to make another estimate and apply the abstract thinking that demonstrates the shift from concrete to representational.

We found that looking at student work enabled teachers to zero in on some nuances of learning and gaps in conceptual understanding that were not evident in summative assessments. This, in turn, made it possible to plan next instructional moves that were strategically targeted to those areas, something that would not have been possible without the close analysis of student work. The 6th grade math example below is an instance of this.

This finding comes with a corollary. As teachers became aware that student work often included richer information about student thinking than was available in their typical summative assessments, they were able to reflect on their own blind spots—what they had been missing before they started looking at student work deeply. For example, this 6th math grade teacher shared how she realized she could have "caught" (her word) the misconceptions of a "higher-level student" earlier if she had analyzed their explanations before she gave the final assessment. She said she usually uses a low score to jar her into action, and because this student was cruising along with high scores, she missed identifying some of the gaps in understanding.

A Classroom Example on Next Instructional Moves: 6th Grade Math

Ms. Watanabe is a seasoned educator with more than 25 years of experience. After teaching kindergarten and 1st grade for many years, Ms. Watanabe made the jump to teach 6th grade math about 10 years ago, when her school expanded from preK–5 to include a middle school division. She teaches three sections of regular math and one advanced math class. The work sample is from her advanced math class that includes students who are certified as academically gifted and also some students who are not officially certified but are seen as students who can be successful in an advanced math course.

Ms. Watanabe presented this student sample to her PLC because she had several personal revelations as a result of looking at this work. Students had been working on understanding and using rational numbers (state standard NC.6.NS.5, "Understand and use rational numbers" [NCDPI, n.d.]). The students completed a 5-page, 15-item multiple-choice summative assessment that tapped into several learning goals about rational numbers: describing quantities having opposite directions or values; describing rational numbers as integers, fractions, and decimals; understanding the absolute value of a rational number as its distance from zero on the number line; and explaining the differences between comparisons involving the absolute value of numbers and comparisons involving the numbers themselves. Ms. Watanabe asks her students to show their work as part of her regular instruction. For this test, she had asked the students to show their reasoning for their answer choices by using an illustration, calculation, or verbal explanation.

Prior to her PLC work, Ms. Watanabe said she would have graded the assessment, recorded it, and moved on with instruction, like many middle school teachers. The pressure to cover content is a real worry, given the time constraints and scheduling of a busy middle school day. The students in this class are typically very successful students, and it is often challenging to extend their learning because of their history of good grades.

Because of her involvement with the PLC, Ms. Watanabe examined the work instead of merely grading it and moving on. She noticed one student seemed more comfortable using illustrations than written explanations to explain his thinking. When she thought more about this, she noticed the student made several careless errors—and those errors corresponded directly to the test items for which there was only minimal sharing of his thought processes and no written explanation. Here is an example:

Student Work 4.6

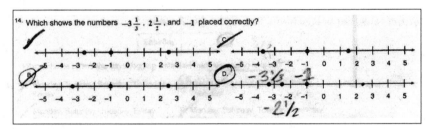

It is clear that the careless error here is merely copying "–2½" onto the number line instead of "2½," a transcription error that by itself may not seem to mean much. But coupled with the observation of the student's approach to the test as a whole, which was to avoid writing if it was possible to explain the work without it, and the observation that test questions with minimal explanations tended to be answered incorrectly, the teacher recognized a pattern. She described the pattern she observed to the student: hurry to get done but make mistakes in the process.

Ms. Watanabe had given students an opportunity to look over their work prior to turning it in, and in fact, she even gave extra time for students to review and make any changes needed before submitting. This student claimed he had looked over it. She decided the feedback to this student—and to others who rush through things—needed to explicitly address how to look over the problems when they are done. It sounded something like, "I can see you have answered all the questions, but I noticed the problems you miss are the same ones where you did not explain your thinking very thoroughly. As you work, try to notice how you think about these problems and make your thinking visible for me. By doing this, you can increase your own awareness and also help me see where you are getting tangled up."

Ms. Watanabe also decided she needed to modify her next instructional moves. She had used peer conferences in the past but thought this group of students might particularly benefit from having an opportunity to confer with each other about their answers before moving into a graded assignment. She felt like these students, despite being in the top of their class, were not able to share their thinking in a way that fully met the learning targets. She reasoned that increasing opportunities to justify an answer would be able to help them become better at self-analysis. Her hope was that the more they could articulate, the easier it would be for them to show this thinking through illustrations, calculations, and explanations.

Finally, Ms. Watanabe pointed out that she usually uses a low score to jar her into looking into problem areas, and because this student was generally doing well, she missed identifying some of his needs: "Because this particular class is generally quite successful, I am missing individual habits of mind that show a breakdown in the mathematical understanding and poor habits of mind." By noticing her own blind spots in this process, she realized she could have identified problems earlier if she had analyzed more of her students' explanations before she gave the final assessment. She is confident that including peer conferencing and analysis of thinking before grading will increase the quality of her students' work.

Missing clues about student thinking in the work of students who usually score well and do well is a common teaching trap that is easy to fall into if we are not vigilant. Looking at student work for evidence of student thinking rather than correctness is the antidote. The idea that there are top students who score well is related to the traditional grading papers mentality. If the name of the game is scoring well, then it follows that students who do are fine. This is not so much wrong as imprecise. Even students who score well may have areas where they can improve that will go unnoticed unless we look at their work for evidence of their thinking.

Summary

Deciding on next instructional moves and giving feedback are both, on average, more difficult for teachers than interpreting student thinking. Teachers with strong content and pedagogical content knowledge are more skilled at taking these next steps than those without. In fact, once a teacher deeply understands students' thinking, a sort of moral imperative arises: What am I going to do about it? We have presented examples of student work and teacher thinking about that work that shows how targeted next steps can meet students right where they are, dealing with the specific needs that arise as students move toward learning goals. The result is a more formative process in the classroom.

 Coach's Corner: Hints for Helping Teachers Learn to Decide on Next Instructional Moves

- Teachers who see learning as a process thrive on identifying strengths, pinpointing areas of need, and approaching the next steps. One even mentioned she liked this because it feels like "a puzzle to solve."
- Teachers who are stronger with content knowledge quickly shift into pedagogy ideas and suggestions when considering next steps and also in collaborating with colleagues. They do not spend a lot of time talking about the student. Instead, they dig deeply into the learning trajectory and their pedagogy and are more hopeful about what is possible. To help a teacher learn how to plan next instructional moves, try to work with content that is an area of strength for her.

 Reflection Questions

1. Which is more difficult for you, providing effective feedback to students or deciding on the next instructional steps you will take after you review student work? What are some of the reasons for your choice?

2. Think of a time when student work on one of your assignments surprised you. Look again at the work itself if you still have it. If not, remind yourself what it looked like and what surprised you. Was there any information in the surprise that would have been useful for you as you planned subsequent instruction? What did you do, and what was the result?

5

Supporting
Professional Development

Looking at student work as part of professional development leads to foundational outcomes for teaching and learning: increased teacher content knowledge; increased teacher understanding of student learning progressions in a content area; improved knowledge of the assessment process; more effective feedback and instructional decisions; and improved assessment practices like specifying clear goals, designing tasks and rubrics that lead to evidence of student thinking, and so on. Professional development based in looking at student work can be particularly powerful because it engages teachers in reflecting on the results of their own instruction and the thinking of students they care about. This is especially true for teachers who want to increase their own knowledge but do not want a program structured by others. Looking at student work activates teachers' interests and intuitive sense of learning goals and criteria. Spending time with the work and with colleagues allows teachers the time and space they need to synthesize and crystallize their observations of student work into understandings they can use to support teaching and learning. It is an inductive, rather than a prescriptive, experience.

Examples of Professional Development Projects Centered on Looking at Student Work

Two major reviews of professional development in formative assessment overall—not just those projects based in looking at student work—converge on a set of characteristics that increase the likelihood that the professional development will be successful (Schneider & Randel, 2010; Trumbull & Gerzon, 2013). Schneider and Randel (2010) identified seven general characteristics important for designing professional development in formative assessment: administrative support, individualization of teachers' professional development learning goals, content knowledge, time, collaboration, coherence, and active learning. Trumbull and Gerzon (2013) identified these features of effective professional development programs in general: intensive and ongoing, connected to practice, collaborative (embedded in a professional learning community), content-focused, adapted to local context, active, systemically supported, and coherent. To these general features they added three additional considerations for professional development in formative assessment: a professional culture for change, learning trajectories of teachers, and formats and strategies parallel to those in the classroom. These are two remarkably similar lists! And you probably noticed that professional development based on looking at student work is particularly attuned to most of these characteristics, especially individualization, content knowledge, collaboration, active learning, and classroom relevance.

Several of the resources we have already cited gave examples of professional development in formative assessment centered specifically on looking at student work (e.g., the Mathematics Learning Community Project [Cleaves & Mayrand, 2011]; the Assessment Work Sample Method [Beesley et al., 2018; Dempsey et al., 2015, 2016]; Collaborative Analysis of Student Work [Langer, Colton, & Goff, 2003]). We have already noted what these projects have in common: a basis in looking at student work, similar teacher learning outcomes (interpreting student thinking, giving effective feedback, deciding on next instructional moves, and supporting professional development), and teacher engagement.

Each project had some unique aspects, as well. In this section, we will briefly describe the structure of two of the projects with published results: the Mathematics Learning Community Project and the Assessment Work Sample Method. Both projects centered on mathematics, the latter on middle school mathematics, specifically. In the next section, we describe the professional learning community project we completed this year, with teachers from a variety of subject areas and grade levels, and continue our use of examples to describe what happened. We hope you will notice that all three of these program descriptions exemplify most of those characteristics and features that are known to help professional development be successful. Further, the use of student work in these projects is the mechanism by which this happens. What could be more tied to a teacher's classroom context than the work done in that very same classroom?

The Mathematics Learning Community Project

The Mathematics Learning Community (MLC) project was designed to help teachers delve into how children understand mathematics (Cleaves & Mayrand, 2011; Massachusetts Department of Elementary and Secondary Education, 2011). The MLCs aimed to give mathematics teachers an opportunity both for collaboration with peers across grade levels and for connecting mathematics content and pedagogy to their own classroom work. MLCs consisted of 7 to 15 members and were co-facilitated by teacher leaders or math coaches. A typical two-hour MLC session followed this agenda (Cleaves & Mayrand, 2011, p. 35):

1. *Mathematical Background* (20 minutes). Teachers study the content background required for the session's math tasks.
2. *Math Metacognition* (25 minutes). Teachers solve math problems and share thought processes and problem solutions.
3. *Looking at Student Work* (50 minutes). Teachers analyze student work using the MLC protocol.
4. *Our Learning* (20 minutes). Teachers practice applying their learning— for example, writing problems that relate the math content to their classroom instruction.
5. *Feedback and Wrap-Up* (5 minutes). Teachers reflect on their learning, using a quick-write, and give feedback about the session.

Notice that the structure of the MLC sessions sets the student work in the context of mathematical content learning. As we have mentioned throughout this book, the deeper one's content knowledge, the more one can gain from looking at student work. The facilitator's materials for each session prescribe math metacognition problems for teachers to solve and student work for teachers to review that are both related to the same math content (Massachusetts Department of Elementary and Secondary Education, 2011).

MLCs use anonymous student work for the Looking at Student Work portion of the session. The idea is to remove any personal feelings of ownership of the teaching behind the student work and to avoid making assumptions MLC teachers might make about students who are known to them. In MLCs, teachers use a protocol for looking at student work (Cleaves & Mayrand, 2011, p. 37):

1. Read the problem and discuss what it is assessing.
2. Solve the problem individually.
3. Share your thinking with a partner.
4. Discuss the mathematics of the problem as a whole group.
5. Look at how students solved the same problem.
6. Identify evidence of understanding by using guiding questions.
7. Discuss evidence of student understanding as a whole group.

MLC facilitators have reported that the biggest obstacles have been finding time and sustaining the MLCs. Administrator support and participation have been key to addressing these obstacles. The program partnered with the Massachusetts Department of Elementary and Secondary Education, the Intel Foundation, and the Noyce foundation in its development. It has since been vetted for inclusion as a program in WestEd's STEMworks database (https://stemworks.wested.org/mathematics-learning-community).

The Assessment Work Sample Method

The Assessment Work Sample Method originated at McREL as part of an Institute of Education Sciences–funded grant to build middle school mathematics teachers' knowledge and skills for implementing high-quality formative assessment (Dempsey et al., 2016). The program was titled Learning to Use Formative Assessment in Mathematics with the Assessment Work Sample Method (AWSM). One of us (Sue) was on the national advisory panel that gave feedback to McREL along the way. We all had a lot of fun talking about our awesome teachers.

The idea was that reviewing and discussing authentic student work would help participating teachers shift from thinking of teaching and teachers' work to thinking of learning and students' work—that is, shift from "instructivist" (Box et al., 2015, p. 972) teaching to more constructivist teaching. Looking at student work was also intended to avoid a problem some professional development has, namely—that many teachers have difficulty connecting things they learn in professional development to their own classroom practice.

McREL recruited teachers to contribute work samples via a structured process. Each work sample contained a cover sheet detailing the teacher's intended goals for the lesson, the type of student knowledge or skill to be developed, criteria for meeting the goals, and other general information about the lesson and assignment. Teachers attached two pieces of student work that met the intended learning goals and two pieces that did not. These work samples helped McREL validate a rubric for rating their quality, important for the professional development study later on, and became some of the anonymous work samples used in the program materials.

The AWSM professional development in formative assessment was built around three dimensions (Beesley et al., 2018): (1) learning goals and task selection, (2) success criteria, and (3) descriptive feedback. The structure included a two-day introductory workshop on formative assessment and eight 45-minute sessions, approximately once a month. Part I of the introductory workshop was about the place of formative assessment in a larger assessment system, emphasizing the role of descriptive feedback and a positive classroom culture in moving learning forward. In Part II, teachers looked at anonymous student work samples, collaboratively examining the alignment of the task to learning goals and discussing the task's mathematics content and cognitive demand. In Part III, teachers analyzed and revised their own instructional unit plans to incorporate what they had just learned about communicating learning expectations, aligning tasks to goals, and building formative assessment opportunities into lessons.

The short sessions were facilitated as teacher learning communities. The facilitator had both mathematics and formative assessment expertise. Sessions one through five were mostly about descriptive feedback, although all topics from the introductory workshop were mentioned, and participants continued to look at anonymous student work samples. In sessions six through eight, participants shared their own student work samples, using the same structure of a cover sheet and four work samples. They presented their work to the group and received feedback, then reflected on their own formative assessment plans and identified next steps for their own learning. In other words, the learning communities modeled the formative assessment process in their work together.

Participants' teacher work samples were used as pre and post measures. They were scored using a rubric with six dimensions (Beesley et al., 2018):

- Focus of the goals on student learning.
- Alignment of learning goals and task.
- Alignment of learning goals and assessment criteria.
- Clarity of the student assessment criteria.
- Feedback type (from evaluative through descriptive).
- Feedback integrates student involvement.

Participants improved on all six dimensions, although the improvement of "focus of the goals on learning" did not reach significance. That dimension was already the strongest at the time of pretesting. The greatest improvements, with huge effect sizes, were for the two aspects of feedback: giving descriptive feedback and involving students.

Common Threads

These program descriptions show that professional development based on looking at student work can be structured in different ways. The student work can be anonymous, belong to the participants, or be both. Despite their differences, these programs had some common threads that are important for us to notice.

First, both professional development programs moved teachers from a focus on instruction and teaching to a focus on moving students along a formative learning cycle—from instructivist to constructivist. Second, and related, student learning goals and success criteria were a major focus in both programs. Third, both programs emphasized the quality of the assignments or tasks students were given and their mathematics content. Fourth, both programs derived their power from the insights teachers gained by looking at student work and inferring student thinking.

Our Professional Development PLCs

We (the authors, Sue and Alice) have worked together for a while to offer professional development on formative assessment. For this book, we decided to redesign some of our professional development to harness the power of looking at student work. Instead of starting with a formal "sit and get" workshop in a large room, this professional development had to fit within a regular school day with teachers who had a full load of teaching and learning going on around the meeting times. As with our previous work together, Sue provided assessment content and support, and Alice did the on-site facilitation work with teachers.

To be as noninvasive as possible, we asked for volunteers and were delighted at the amount of people who responded. The first sessions were a wonderful mix of small groups sprinkled across the regular school day that met almost weekly across two months. Most participants were able to attend between five and eight sessions, depending on their own personal circumstances.

Alice provided some direct instruction in the first session, to build context for the project and build background in formative assessment using Sue's materials. In this session, Alice used the poetry work samples we described in Chapter 2 to generate conversations around four purposes of looking at student work: inferring student thinking, providing effective feedback, deciding on next instructional moves, and supporting professional development. The groups only had about an hour to meet, so Alice wanted to make sure the chunks of formative assessment content were not only relevant but also digestible for teachers who had other things going on. The sample student poems generated lively conversations and helped begin the reflective practice and collaborative work that would be the foundation for this professional development.

After digging into the student work samples, Alice had the participants think about kinds of work from their own classrooms that would be useful to examine in a project like this. She encouraged teachers to identify open-ended tasks, writing, journaling, projects, and anything that could show student thinking in a meaningful way. Tasks that required lower-level thinking or restating of facts would not allow us to have rich discussions about student thinking and learning the way some of the other assignments would. Participants were encouraged to think across content areas as well as consider a variety of samples types to bring to the group.

For the second session, Alice decided to dig deeper into providing useful feedback, because that would be important to the discussions moving forward. She used Sue's micro view feedback guidelines (see Figure 3.3) with participants and had them practice improving feedback on one of the "Cats and Dogs" persuasive essays, written by a classmate of the student whose essay you read in Chapter 2. Then, participants used that same process to provide descriptive feedback on one piece of student work they had brought to discuss with the group.

A majority of our participants had never had any formal professional development about effective feedback or the formative assessment cycle. At first, some teachers were a little reluctant to share their thinking around the student work. Practicing on the "Cats and Dogs" essay and using the micro view feedback analysis criteria for support helped give participants the confidence they needed to give descriptive feedback a try.

Conversational and collaborative professional development was new to many of them as well. This was energizing and challenging at the same time. Participants were used to professional development of the "sit and get" variety. They were not used to the demands of responding to such open-ended tasks themselves. It took a few sessions for them to become more comfortable with the process and with each other. The groups were small, so engagement and participation of all members was expected; sitting back silently in a group of four people does not go unnoticed. Because most of them had not spent a lot of time sharing pedagogical thinking with one another, things were a little clunky at first. Even so, the exit tickets at the end of these sessions included excitement and positivity from the participants. Ms. Sandoval noted, "I enjoyed a pleasant meeting with people interested in the work. The fellowship was good." Ms. Trent wrote, "I have gained perspective and inspiration from this."

To help structure and guide the conversations in the third session, Alice created the five-thought organizer in Figure 5.1. It is designed to be a tool for organizing thinking around student work samples of any kind in any grade level, with a focus on the four purposes we have already described for doing so. In session three, teachers worked through the organizer in real time in the sessions, but for the following meetings, Alice realized it made sense to have them use this to gather their thoughts *prior* to meeting so all the time could be spent on talking and collaborating around the student work samples.

The standard is purposefully placed at the top of the organizer to center teachers' thinking on what they want students to know and be able to do. This provides a clear focus for conversation about students' work and helps the teacher unpack both student and teacher thinking around one clear idea. This focus is especially important because we only had 45–60 minutes for talking about multiple work samples. Without the standard, the conversations can quickly stall out or be nonproductive. The rest of the organizer is

Figure 5.1

Five-Thought Organizer

What was the learning target/standard for this work?

Notice: Describe what you observe in this work. What do you notice is going well and/or needs attention? What do you wonder?	**Analyze:** (Content, Student, Pedagogy, Assessment) What does this work tell you? What can we infer?
Feedback: What feedback would be useful for this student to feed learning forward? **Tip:** Consider the success criteria that align with the learning target for this lesson.	**Action:** What could be one next instructional move for this student?

Reflections:
What am I noticing about myself/my own thinking during this process?

structured to pull people through the process of looking at student work. Starting very simply with "What do you notice?" and moving into analysis, feedback, and then finally what actions would be supportive of this student, the organizer itself becomes a map for conversations. The Reflections section of the organizer was designed to capture thinking from the teachers. This was useful for Alice as a facilitator and also gave a window into the evolution of ideas from the participants. Teachers' reflections were not shared with the group unless they wanted to share them.

Early in the project, teachers revealed how this project was affecting their thinking. "I am learning how valuable it is to take the extra time for kids to process and how that leads to me processing differently. This has changed my lens on student work," shared Ms. Hamilton. At this point, we had expected participants to reference using standards as a guide for feedback, but instead, participants were reporting how looking at student work was helping them shift perspective from what they were teaching to what students were learning. This clear evidence of the instructivist-to-constructivist shift was exciting to watch!

As the sessions progressed, Alice would send a reminder e-mail with the organizer and ask participants to select a sample, reflect on the work sample and gather their thoughts, and then bring the student work sample and the organizer to the meetings. Some people brought multiple work samples because they were excited to share or because they wanted some thinking from the group on specific examples. For the sake of time, Alice sometimes asked them to select the one sample that surprised them in some way that they would really be able to chat about. This helped participants move away from always sharing the most difficult student in the class or the most perfect student in the class. The range of samples helped people see ways to reach all students and, while they certainly talked about the lower and upper range of achievement, they also were able to dig into the middle range.

For the most part, the conversations flowed more naturally with each meeting. Teachers who had not always started with the standards started bringing their resources and clearly stated the standards in our conversations and on the organizers. The confidence of the participants grew, and they were able to contribute more and more in each session. The next example shows how this happened with one teacher.

A Classroom Example on Growing Teacher Confidence: Kindergarten Writing

When we first started our project, Ms. Rodriguez was an active listener in our sessions but often held back when sharing student work. She shared that she was not normally a passive participant in professional development, but she was doing a lot of "processing and thinking as we talk and I feel like I am learning." She continued to come to the sessions, listen, add thinking, and stay engaged.

Several sessions into the project, Ms. Rodriguez brought a writing sample from a student. She selected this piece to share with the group because she wanted input on what next steps to suggest for this writer. She knew the student was trying to say, "I am hiking with my cousins," and the picture she drew matched her message.

Student Work 5.1a

Student Work 5.1b

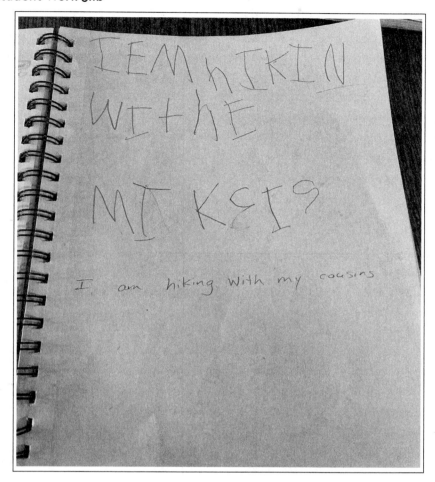

The state standards (NCDPI, n.d.) were SL.K.5, *"Add drawings or other visual displays to descriptions as desired to provide additional detail,"* and L.K.2, *"Demonstrate command of the conventions of standard English capitalization, punctuation, and spelling when writing; demonstrate proficiency within the K–1 conventions continuum." The learning target for today's lesson was "We can write about a true thing that happened to us." The success criteria or look-fors were "My words show the sounds I hear, I use finger spaces, I put periods at the end of the sentence, I tell back what I wrote, I use sight words, and my picture supports the writing."*

Ms. Rodriguez recognized this student had words that matched the picture, was showing evidence of phonemic awareness, had used some finger spaces but not consistently, and could tell what she wrote. After further thought, she said, "I think she is on track." The group contributed some thinking that could be useful feedback based on the sample and the learning target. It sounded something like this: "I can see from your writing you were able to sound out the words. Do you think you could work to use a finger space more consistently? Also, what goes at the end of a sentence? Do you think you could practice using punctuation each time?"

Ms. Rodriguez went on to think about how to support this student moving forward. She had ideas but could not land on what should be the very next step. She shared her frustrations with the group. She had already taught them finger spacing and punctuation. Why weren't they using it, and how could she be helpful?

One of her colleagues, Ms. Griffith, shared that she also has this problem with her kindergarten writers. She shared that it is not unusual to have to teach this over and over again for students to actually "get it." Ms. Fiorenza echoed that she also has the same issue regularly. One thing Ms. Griffith usually does to address this is teach students to explicitly count out the number of words they are trying to write and then double check to see if that is the number on the paper. In this case, "I am hiking with my cousins" would be six words on the paper.

Sharing a common frustration with the group helped Ms. Rodriguez realize this issue is not unique to her students. By normalizing this common problem, the group not only helped Ms. Rodriguez realize this is typical but also helped her move into next steps with this student and additional students who are having this problem. "It was so helpful for me to hear that I need to focus on even more details such as numbers of words in sentences," she said." I appreciate being reminded of how we need to break it down for our youngest writers."

The collaborative nature of the conversations around student work is what ultimately helped all the participants increase their comfort level for sharing and supported their professional growth. Alice eased this process by inviting other participants to chime in and help problem solve. Participants' comfort level for asking the group for ideas actively increased across the meetings. Most of the time, the teachers exhibited a mindset of learning together and from one another. They enjoyed spending the time talking about teaching and learning. The process was working for them, and their ability to reflect and collaborate was increasing their professional thinking.

Sometimes teachers did get stuck. When that happened, Alice would gently redirect with questioning that related back to the success criteria and intended learning for the standard. When time allowed, Alice could also help teachers participate in role-plays to practice feedback and help teachers consider what it looks and sounds like. Here is one example of that.

A Classroom Example on Role-Playing Feedback: 4th Grade English Language Arts

Ms. Feinstein is a seasoned educator who is teaching 4th grade English language arts. She is part of the team that includes a teacher who teaches science and social studies and another who teaches math. Ms. Feinstein was a very willing participant to share student work and unpack her thinking with the group. The state standard she was teaching (NCDPI, n.d.) was L.4.5, "Demonstrate understanding of figurative language, word relationships, and nuances in word meanings." The learning target for today's lesson was "I can use details from the text to draw conclusions and make inferences." Success criteria included "I will identify and explain figurative language used in poems by making inferences, I will refer to the text to prove my answer, and I will explain my answer fully."

This assignment included a variety of questions centered around two Shel Silverstein poems, "Hippo's Hope" and "Recipe for a Hippopotamus Sandwich." Ms. Feinstein had been working with students to "prove their answers"—her term for supporting assertions with details from the text—by referencing the text. She explained to us that on the first try, this student didn't tell where the information was coming from: "She essentially was just making things up. I told her I needed to see the proof and explicit details and words from the text and then sent her back to keep working." After the student went back and continued to work, Ms. Feinstein checked back in with her and found her work improved. The work now showed appropriate use of the chart—"It says/I say/So I infer"—and referenced the text explicitly in the first column. This is more of what Ms. Feinstein was looking for.

Student Work 5.2

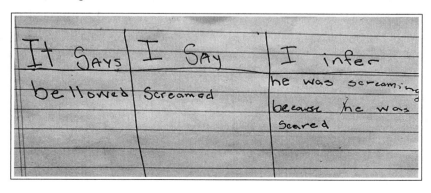

Knowing that students need feedback even when they are correct, Ms. Feinstein asked what exactly she should say to this student because she wanted to make sure she understood how much better the second attempt was. To help with this, Alice played the student and Ms. Feinstein practiced. Ms. Feinstein used the success criteria to come up with her feedback, and they role-played for the group. It sounded like this:

> Ms. Feinstein: Your second attempt at this question showed me more of your thinking. Your previous example was not clear, but now you have made me understand.
>
> Alice/Pretend Student: Thank you.
>
> Ms. Feinstein: Your example was specific and clear. I can tell you know what the word *bellowed* means. What helped you the second time you tried?
>
> Alice/Pretend Student: I was able to use my chart and write my thinking more clearly.
>
> Ms. Feinstein: Yes, you stuck to the process, and I can see your thinking about the poem now. Keep using this as you practice making inferences on other poems, too!

Role-playing what feedback looks and sounds like not only helped us practice but also helped build a picture for the other teachers in the session. At the end of the session, the other participants said the role-play example brought clarity to their own thoughts about how to phrase things for students.

In some cases, looking at student work helped teachers see that the problem was trying to include too many learning targets in each lesson and feedback session, as in the example below. Once teachers narrowed the targets, there was a sense of clarity—and relief!

A Classroom Example on Too Many Targets: Kindergarten Social Studies

It is not uncommon for teachers to get a little tangled up and not know when or how to give feedback when the issue is not always the feedback itself . . . it is too many targets! In one of our very first sessions, Ms. Tyler brought a civics and government work sample to the group.

In this lesson, Ms. Tyler invoked one state standard with two clarifying objectives for civics and government (NCDPI, n.d.): K.C&G.1, "Understand the roles of a citizen"; K.C&G.1.1, "Exemplify positive relationships through fair play and friendship"; and K.C&G.1.2, "Explain why citizens obey rules in the classroom, school, home, and neighborhood." The learning target for today's lesson was "We can show how to be a good citizen."

Their assignment was to draw an example of good citizenship on a paper that read, "I can be a good citizen." Lloyd drew a picture of helping his brother get up as a way to show good citizenship. He drew two smiling people in his picture. Because Lloyd is not able to write full sentences, he dictated his work to Ms. Tyler, who jotted his thinking on his paper.

Student Work 5.3

When Alice initially asked Ms. Tyler to talk about the context of this work and what she was looking for—even if just a general notion of what went well and what areas would need support—she shared the following things that she was looking for:

- *Do the hands have fingers?*
- *How does the student hold the crayon or marker?*
- *Can the student speak one word for each printed word (voice-print match)?*

- *Was the paper oriented the correct way?*
- *Can the student write their name or just the beginning letter?*

When Alice asked her what standard this work sample aligned with, she said, "They were learning about being good citizens." Alice says, "Having watched Ms. Tyler teach, I know she is professional, plans well, and regularly approaches instruction by looking at the whole child. In no way would I question what is possible in her classroom. In this case, however, as we took a deep dive into student work, we were able to peel back some layers that could help refine her feedback to students."

Ms. Tyler was thinking about feedback in terms of writing and language arts, but the standard was related to civics. As the group considered what might be useful feedback for this student, they felt overwhelmed with all of the possible responses. So Alice led them back to the standard Ms. Tyler originally wanted to address. That civics standard could be pretty complex for kindergartners: "Good citizen" is an abstract concept. Once the group was clear on the mismatch between the standard and the success criteria, they were able to begin to consider relevant writing and language arts standards that would align specifically to this assignment. The first thing they noticed was that there were a lot of them. Some of the possibilities they identified were as follows (NCDPI, n.d.):

> W.K.1 Use a combination of drawing, dictating, and writing to compose opinion pieces in which they tell a reader the topic or the name of the book they are writing about and state an opinion or preference about the topic or book.
>
> a. With guidance and support from adults, respond to questions and suggestions from adults and/or peers and add details to strengthen writing as needed.
>
> SL.K.5 Add drawings or other visual displays to descriptions as desired to provide additional detail.
>
> L.K.2 Demonstrate command of the conventions of standard English capitalization, punctuation, and spelling when writing; demonstrate proficiency within the K–1 conventions continuum.

In addition, because kindergarten teachers are such wonderful kid-watchers, it was easier at first for the group to focus on student behaviors instead of student thinking. It can be difficult to "see" the thinking of our most emergent learners. The behaviors, the writing and language skills, and the civic concepts are all important, but in order to give effective feedback on this specific learning target, they had to get very, very clear on what they were looking for. Together, the group looked back at the clarifying objectives for the civic standard about good citizenship (NCDPI, n.d.): K.C&G.1.1, "Exemplify positive relationships through fair play and friendship," and K.C&G.1.2, "Explain why citizens obey rules in the classroom, school, home, and neighborhood."

Ms. Tyler thought his work suggested that Lloyd was on track about showing positive relationships, but maybe he could add an explanation on why this is important in order to meet the second objective. Also, she realized she would still be looking for the language arts skills, but for feedback, she would only focus on the civics standard for this session. This seemed much more doable than giving feedback and next steps on civics standards as well as writing and language standards. What a relief!

At the beginning of the next session, Ms. Tyler told Alice she "had a revelation" since the last meeting. She said:

> I went back and looked through the work samples again and had a whole new perspective. I noticed how a lot of them focused on one person . . . it was important at that time of year [the beginning of the year] for them to learn their new friends' names. I'm thinking now at this point in the year [second semester] I would have asked them for a broader way to think about being a good citizen—is it being nice to more than just one person?

This example of narrowing and clarifying learning intentions and criteria, based in looking at a simple drawing of a little boy helping his brother get up, took Ms. Tyler and her PLC colleagues through discussions of content, pedagogy, student behavior, and feedback. In addition to illustrating our smaller point about some lessons having too many standards, we think it illustrates our larger theme about the power of looking at student work. From seemingly simple evidence of learning, profound discussions can happen when teachers look at student work through the lenses of content and pedagogy and their experience with children.

Here is another example, with older students, where a teacher experienced professional growth in understanding the importance of clear learning goals. As with the previous example, other issues of student thinking and writing are intermingled, as well. Looking at student work sometimes raises as many questions as it answers.

A Classroom Example on Multiple Learning Goals: 6th Grade Social Studies

Ms. Marshall had been working on geography and environmental literacy with her 6th grade students. State standards (NCDPI, n.d.) included 6.G.1,

"Understand geographic factors that influenced the emergence, expansion, and decline of civilizations, societies, and regions over time (i.e., Africa, Asia, Europe, and the Americas)," and 6.G.1.2, *"Explain factors that influenced the movement of people, goods, and ideas and the effects of that movement on societies and regions over time (e.g. scarcity of resources, conquests, desire for wealth, disease, and trade)."* The learning target for today's lesson was *"We can explain how North and South America became populated by the first Americans."*

Students had learned about the factors that influenced movement through several lessons that included reading materials on the topic. For this particular work sample, students were asked to do a quick-write for an exit ticket. The quick-write needed to summarize the reading for that day and address the question *"How did North and South America become populated by the first Americans?"* Ms. Marshall was looking for students to use relevant information from the reading to explain their thinking and to include factors that influenced their movement. Here are some samples of the exit tickets she received.

When Ms. Marshall looked at the responses, she grew concerned. The first student had pulled his answer directly from the text. Because of this, she wondered about his real understanding of the materials. Upon further analysis, she noted that while he quoted some of the expected information, he really missed an important chunk of it. *"I am thinking he was satisfied to have answered but was not really concerned with a depth of answer."* She wanted to work her feedback around going deeper and expanding ideas and realized she needed to convince him he should reread his responses and reflect on how well he addressed the question. Even students who did not quote the text verbatim gave simple, literal answers like in the three samples shown in Student Works 5.4, 5.5, and 5.6.

Part of the issue could be addressed by writing more precise prompts. For example, instead of "How did North and South America become populated by the first Americans?" the question might have been phrased "How did North and South America become populated by the first Americans? Why did they come? Name and explain several factors behind the migration of the first Americans." As we discussed in Chapter 2, the questions and tasks you set before students will affect the responses they give, and in most cases you will get what you ask for.

In addition to sharpening their question-writing skills, the group chatted about the more general issue of students giving minimal, literal answers to text-based questions. It became apparent this phenomenon—answering questions by pulling information verbatim, or almost verbatim, from a text

Student Work 5.4

> Because this was the time of the ice
> age and so every thing was frozen
> so they crossed this bridge that
> leaded them in to north america
> then they just started to adapt
> there

Student Work 5.5

> The americans migrated and
> had more kids. They made
> more settlements and kept migratin

Student Work 5.6

> Americans came from Europe,
> Africa, or the South Pacific,
> across a land bridge.

—happens in a variety of grades and content areas. Ms. Green, a 3rd grade teacher who was in the PLC, said she had the same issues. Students would answer a question with a surface-level response, but they often miss a large chunk of content or big idea from the lesson. A 6th grade teacher said she notices this in her science written work and quick-writes, too.

This conversation led the group to a deeper discussion around feedback. Did this student need more scaffolding with content, or did this student need something else? The group considered the content lens—what exactly did cause North and South America to become populated by the first Americans—but the literacy lens also appeared again. Was this a content issue, or was this a written expression issue?

It became apparent from the PLC conversation that writing in the content area was emerging as a need across multiple grade levels at this school. If Ms. Green was seeing this in 3rd grade, then chances are there were weaknesses prior to that. Ms. Green suggested they consider some possible vertical planning discussions to see how different grade levels are approaching writing in the content area. "Maybe this is something to discuss with our leadership team," she said. How was content-area writing taught in the younger grades, and was anyone having particular success? What needed to happen in the middle school to build on this and help students head off to high school as effective writers? These important questions emerged from the conversation that day. Without explicitly addressing the writing component, it would be difficult to decipher whether the student needed more information related to the content or needed explicit writing instruction, or both.

As you can see, looking at student work in small groups of four teachers, from different content areas and grade levels, set in motion professional development in a variety of areas for our PLC participants. They talked about the nature of assignments and assessments, learning targets and success criteria, feedback, instructional decisions, and content issues. They voiced their professional learning needs and their feelings about them. There was a lot of sharing. Each teacher learned different things and took away different ideas about what to try next. The one thing they had in common was a commitment to continuing to look at student work for evidence of student thinking and increasing motivation to act on that evidence in their classrooms.

 **Summary**

Professional development based on looking at student work is a powerful and enjoyable way to foster teachers' growth in formative assessment. Specific formative assessment skills that are strengthened include clarifying learning targets and success criteria, interpreting student thinking, providing effective feedback, and using evidence of current student learning to inform next instructional moves. Looking at student work is a powerful way to scaffold the learning of all teachers, because there is a way in for everyone: All teachers have students, and they all do work. Concrete examples of student work help teachers with less background knowledge in relevant content and pedagogy to get a vision of what they are trying to learn professionally—to set a professional learning goal. Teachers with more background knowledge in relevant content and pedagogy can move quickly from looking at student work to questions about feedback and instructional next steps. Group problem solving often happens, becoming the "rising tide that raises all boats." And, in addition, teachers report they enjoy looking at student work; they find it fun. Or maybe that is not "in addition" at all. Maybe it is part of the reason looking at student work makes for effective professional development.

Coach's Corner: Hints for Facilitating a PLC Based on Looking at Student Work

Having Conversations Around Student Work

- Participants often enjoy repeat use of the five-thought organizer in each session. They feel like they know how to organize their thoughts.

- Some participants may struggle with making inferences around content and crafting feedback. Scaffold and redirect them when they veer off to avoid irrelevant "bird walks."

- Looking at student work is an authentic mechanism for professional development. It makes for conversations that are much easier to digest than a full workshop on formative assessment or feedback. Therefore, while it is a great method for all teachers, it may be an especially effective way into professional development in formative assessment for teachers with less background knowledge and skills.

- Not everything can be tackled in one session. Make notes to help guide and prioritize conversations.

- In conversations with a cross-section of grades and subjects, there are moments where two different thinkers come together to problem solve organically.

- Providing time and space for people to reflect and talk is part of high-quality professional development. It can change mindsets much quicker than a PowerPoint presentation.

- Important thinking can take place in the space of vulnerability if the group climate is focused on growth and learning.

- Analysis of student work should invoke issues of content, pedagogy, assessment, and students. There may be a tendency to discuss student issues alone, or discuss the student and not the work, and avoid discussing issues of content, pedagogy, and assessment inherent in the work. Use open-ended, facilitative questions to ensure a balanced discussion.

Handling a Range of Teacher Backgrounds in Content and Pedagogy

- Some teachers may get stuck analyzing the student and not the actual work and its relation to the learning targets, standards, and content. We suggest gently redirecting them with questions that relate back to the success criteria and student learning. With this scaffolding, they can be more successful.

- Some teachers may not be used to discussing student work and be reluctant to share their thinking or want to say the right thing. From the beginning, establish a PLC culture that is about learning, not evaluating. Use specific questions first that require less risk to answer, then branch to more open questions.

- Teachers with weaker understanding of content and pedagogy are able to build on ideas from others in the group. Learning from more experienced peers works for adults as well as children!

- Teachers who feel threatened by others in the room will need explicit protocols and support to share thinking and make themselves vulnerable in conversations. The five-thought organizer provided a structure and an outline for us and was a simple way to organize teachers' preparation for and participation in the sessions. More complex protocols are available from the National School Reform Faculty, many of which are available for free online at https://nsrfharmony.org/protocols/. The Tuning Protocol and the Standards in Practice Protocol are especially suitable for looking at student work.

- Teachers with high self-efficacy enjoy opportunities to reflect and openly talk about their work. Looking at student work gradually makes this possible for teachers who are not as confident, and they open up more as a result of the low-stakes conversations.

- In discussion, a teacher may reveal glaring misconceptions about instruction. This is a difficult situation for a coach in a small-group setting with peers and administrators. Have a private conversation with the teacher, outside the PLC session.

 Reflection Questions

1. What are your plans for professional development using student work? Are you a teacher who has wondered how to get more information from the wealth of evidence your students create every day in your classroom? Are you a coach or facilitator who would like to lead a PLC group? What have you learned in this chapter that will help you take your next steps?

2. Are you ready to try a mini-session? Grab an interested colleague. Each of you should select an assignment for which some of the student work surprised you. Independently, each of you should complete the five-thought organizer, and then set aside some uninterrupted time to discuss what you see in the work in light of the learning goal and criteria. Be sure to talk about the issues of content, pedagogy, assessment, and the student that are reflected in the work. Take stock when you finish. What did you learn? Would you like to do more?

3. What barriers do you envision might get in the way of your plans for professional development based on looking at student work? How might you overcome them?

6

Looking at Student Work in a New Way

True confession time. One of the authors (Sue) was the student teacher in the story in Chapter 1. As the story shows, Sue began her career in education thinking that looking at student work was a chore to be accomplished, and that the main point of it was grading papers to find out how "right" students were in their answers. Over the course of a career looking into student work more deeply, she has come to see it as a gold mine of information about student learning and a foundational source of information for formative assessment.

Alice's journey is similar. Early in her career, Alice would assign and assess and move on because that is what she thought teachers had to do. It never occurred to her that the information the students were sharing with her was important to her next steps with instruction and, more important, their learning! As Maya Angelou said, "Do the best you can until you know better. Then when you know better, do better." Now when Alice looks at student work, she looks through a lens of curiosity and wonder. She tries to figure out what the work is telling her and how she can work alongside the student to create ways for learning to continue.

Therefore, we have written this book together to invite you, our readers, to take a journey we have taken ourselves. We promise you it is an exciting thing to do, and it will change your approach to education. You will move, if you haven't already, from someone who sees teaching as imparting information *to* students to someone who sees teaching as constructing meaning *with* students by finding out how they are thinking and working with them from that place.

In this chapter, we extend the thinking we began in Chapters 2 through 5 and suggest some steps you might take on this journey. All of them center on student work: clarify learning goals, increase the quality of classroom assessments, deepen your content and pedagogical knowledge, study student work with colleagues, and involve students in the formative learning cycle.

Clarify Learning Goals

Looking at student work deeply means looking inside kids' heads to see what they think you wanted them to learn. If the learning goal was not about learning, but rather about following directions (e.g., "Go on the internet, find five facts about grizzly bears, and copy them onto a poster"), looking at student work will give you information about compliance. If the learning goal was intended to be about learning but was not clear, looking at student work most likely will also give you information about compliance. We saw an example of this in Chapter 2, with the "Cats and Dogs" paragraph. The intended learning, to develop persuasive writing skills, was not clear to students, who saw the assignment as learning to write a paragraph according to a formula.

Try a little exercise. Alone if you must, but with a colleague if you can, examine student work from a lesson or assignment that did not go as well as you had hoped. Perhaps most of the student work was mediocre when you expected better. Perhaps, as for the "Cats and Dogs" paragraphs, most of the students' work was eerily similar, when you expected differences or even a little creativity. Perhaps the students didn't seem interested in an assignment that you thought would interest them.

Use the five-thought organizer (see Figure 5.1) to look at and reflect on the student work. Pay special attention to what the assignment showed students thought they were supposed to learn—the "Where am I going?" portion of the formative learning cycle. Look at the standard or learning target you specified and compare what it says to what it seems the students were thinking. Is there a match? Did the students have something to aim for? At this point, you may think of some ways in which the learning goals could have been clearer. You may be able to use this information for your current students, depending on where in their learning trajectory they are at the moment. And you certainly can use this information to think more clearly about the learning goals the next time you teach this same content.

Second, think about how you presented the target to the students before you gave the assignment. Were you clear in your explanation? Did you check for understanding? Did you give students success criteria—and if so, did they use them as they worked? If not, do you need to teach students how to use success criteria?

The third aspect of clarifying learning targets is to make sure that the work—the assignment or assessment—you give students to do is a spot-on match with what they are supposed to be learning. This is important enough that it deserves its own section.

Increase the Quality of Classroom Assessments

Students will get some of their vision about what they are supposed to be learning from what you ask them to do. Mismatched assignments can contribute to unclear goals. For example, suppose you told students they are going to be learning about Hamlet's state of mind at the beginning of Shakespeare's play, but today's classroom work centers on reading Act I, Scene ii, aloud. If students were to conclude from their work what they were supposed to be learning, without reference to what you may have told them, they would probably think that they were supposed to be learning how to do dramatic reading or perhaps how to pronounce Elizabethan English. Likely, those students would have been concentrating more on their pronunciation and their handling of the Shakespearean verses than on how Hamlet was revealing his state of mind at the beginning of the play.

Our typical approach to this issue in the past would have been to suggest a professional development focus on assessment. Of course, that is still a possibility. But you may find, as did many of the teachers we worked with, that looking at student work and focusing on what students are thinking first, and reaching the conclusion that you may want to look at the quality of your assessments as a by-product of that work, may be more productive. At that point, teachers are raising questions about assessment, and "need to know" becomes "want to know."

If you do decide to focus on assessment quality, two easy-to-read resources by one of the authors (Sue) approach assessment in a way that coordinates well with the student work approach we advocate here. One is *How to Design Questions and Tasks to Assess Student Thinking* (Brookhart, 2014), and the other is *How to Create and Use Rubrics for Formative Assessment and Grading* (Brookhart, 2013).

Or it may be that you want to approach all these outcomes more organically, beginning with a PLC based in looking at student work, using the five-thought organizer (Figure 5.1) or some other method, and see where it leads you. You might, as our teachers did, end up focusing a bit on all four outcomes (quality of assignments and student thinking, effective feedback, next instructional moves, and professional development). Or you might end up selecting one of these four as a first area of focus; if you do that, highlighting the quality of assessments would be a good first choice.

Deepen Your Content and Pedagogical Knowledge

Both Alice and Sue have done numerous professional development workshops on questioning skills. One of us remembers doing a brief breakout session on questioning as part of a larger professional development conference. A young elementary school teacher stayed after the session to talk. She said she knew she needed to get better at asking questions that elicited student thinking, but she shared that she was having trouble doing it in science. She said, "I can't figure out how to word the questions. For example, I know that 'Why does the cork float?' could lead to a parroted explanation from the textbook. But all I can think to do is say something like 'Why do you think the cork will float?'" She put air quotes around "do you think," letting me know she realized that was a lame addition that wouldn't really get students to think any deeper.

"Well," I said, "I can help you with some general suggestions, but you need deep content knowledge to write good questions, and science is not an area of deep content knowledge for me." Her face fell. She realized I had just hit the nail on the head. That was the problem; science was not a strong suit for her, and she knew it. For some teachers, I would simply recommend that they invest some time in learning more about the content they teach. With the advent of the internet, there are myriad ways to do that, in addition to the old-school ways like reading books or taking classes. But for this brand-new teacher of a self-contained elementary classroom, deepening content knowledge in all the subject areas she taught was not a realistic thing to ask. We talked for a while, and I ended up suggesting that she find a colleague who does have deep knowledge in science and, in trade for some help in another area—in her case, it would be language arts, where she did excel—get some help with science.

Another aspect of content and pedagogical knowledge that is very important for interpreting student thinking is understanding typical learning progressions within the content area you teach. In some areas, we know a lot about how students typically progress. For example, we know that students usually understand multiplication as repeated addition before they come to a more multiplicative understanding, such as might be shown in an array. Another area where a lot is known about how students typically progress is early literacy. You can find, for example, charts of successively more sophisticated student writing that will help you plan instruction in that area. But in some areas, there is relatively little accessible, published work about typical student learning progressions. In these areas, your teaching experience can be a good source of information. When you have taught this concept before, how have students typically progressed? What understandings came easily to them? What understandings took more time, instruction, or both?

Study Student Work with Colleagues

We are not the first to say this, nor will we be the last, but here is our advice: Make time. Make time to study student work with colleagues. The benefits will be more than worth the time you invest. You will enjoy it, and if you approach it seriously, we can almost guarantee that you will improve the quality of your assignments, the depth of your interpretation of student work, the effectiveness of your feedback, and the appropriateness of your next instructional decisions.

As you know, we recommend you use a professional learning community format—that is, some sort of collegial learning group—as did all the projects we reported in this book, including our own. We recommend that participation is by choice. The obvious reason is that engagement is important, of course. Beyond that, however, participants will need to set professional learning goals and travel in a formative learning cycle toward them. By definition, one has to be aiming for something in order for it to be a goal. The old adage

"You can lead a horse to water, but you can't make it drink" may come to mind here, and it's true. However, looking at student work does have some drawing power, and you may be able to interest people in looking at student work with you if you give them a little demonstration of what it is like.

Involve Students in the Formative Learning Cycle

Chapter 3 described the formative learning cycle (see Figure 3.1). The three questions in Figure 3.1 show how scholars whose main concerns are feedback and formative assessment have described the process (e.g., Hattie & Timperley, 2007; Sadler, 1989). However, educational psychologists express the same concepts in the language of self-regulation of learning and, to the extent that teachers, classmates, and instructional materials also help students make meaning, the co-regulation of learning (Andrade & Brookhart, 2020). In other words, self-regulated learners follow the process diagrammed here as the formative learning cycle whether you or they are aware of it or not.

Therefore, we recommend that you intentionally plan lessons with clear learning targets and criteria, communicate them to students, and have them refer to them as they do their work (Moss & Brookhart, 2019). We expect that this will lead to more thoughtful student work that will give you more to work with as you pursue looking at student work more intentionally. Further information about using learning targets with students may be found in *Learning Targets: Helping Students Aim for Understanding in Today's Lesson* (Moss & Brookhart, 2012).

The Role of Coaches and Facilitators

The Coach's Corner sections in each chapter have featured a gentle approach. Guiding and questioning learners in a safe collegial PLC environment devoted to looking at student work has led to more learning, in our experience, than many if not most of the workshops we have presented over our careers.

We recommend coaches let go of the idea that they must know everything. Being the expert in the room is not possible or needed. No coach, for example, can be an expert in learning progressions in every content area and grade level. It is more important for a coach to understand the formative assessment process and help guide teachers to their own revelations. The coach is like the oil in a machine that keeps everything moving. That comes in the form of providing safe spaces for conversations, creating schedules that allow collaborative work and talk, being a facilitator of professional discourse, and helping people poke around and wrestle with ideas that will help them evolve. In other words, the role of the coach is to help the teachers in the PLC move through their own formative learning cycles as they pursue professional learning goals based on looking at student work.

The Role of Building and District Leaders

In Chapter 5, we showed how studies of professional development in general, and professional development in formative assessment specifically, are effective if (and, sometimes, only if) building administrators are supportive. That of course includes administrative functions like scheduling support that gives teachers space and time to meet together, support for any needed materials, and so on. But we have found the game is changed when the principal becomes the leading learner and focuses on what the students are doing (Brookhart & Moss, 2013).

"Being the leading learner" means just what it says. Building principals who do more than *allow others* to learn by looking at student work, actively learning from doing it themselves, lead buildings where teachers learn more about formative assessment. Building principals who pass off responsibilities for learning about formative assessment to others, not so much. For example, we once met monthly with a group of principals in one school district who were learning about formative assessment. One of the principals could be counted on to make sure he got a copy of all of the handouts, then turn and give them—without looking at them—to his assistant principal and say, "See that the teachers get copies of these." Every. Single. Month. Guess whose building did not make much progress in formative assessment that year?

Further, building principals who understand formative assessment lead the process better than those who don't. This is more than "Do as I say, not as I do." After all, you wouldn't hire a principal who didn't know anything about instruction to lead a building. Why do people expect that a principal can lead successfully without knowing anything about assessment or about student work?

Building principals can take a leading-learner stance to formative assessment in general, and looking at student work in particular, in two major ways. First, the principal can remember that the purpose of a PLC dedicated to looking at student work is formative, for both the teachers and students and, if he or she is a participant, the administrator. There should be nothing tied to teacher evaluation in the mix. Second, the formative purpose is best served when everyone looks at what the students are doing first and other things (instruction, classroom environment, materials) second. The principal can lead by example in both of those ways.

In our recent PLCs based on looking at student work, having the administrators in the process was useful. The administrative team attended the PLC sessions that were held during the regular school day. Their presence alongside the teachers created an opportunity to build true learning communities. Looking at student work this way led to authentic conversations about teaching and learning, as opposed to formal conversations around evaluations.

During one PLC meeting, an administrator particularly appreciated the conversations around success criteria. After a lively conversation around the "Cats and Dogs" paragraph, one administrator commented, "Sometimes checking off the boxes in a rubric can get in the way of actually learning what is important." This comment helped open the door for the teachers to try new instructional moves and really examine with a fresh lens what they are asking students to know and be able to do within individual lessons. Another administrator shared his takeaway: "You get what you ask for." This led participants to talk more about standards and how explicit they need to be with the success criteria.

Regarding the role of district leaders in supporting professional learning, we have been very intrigued by the recent work of Farrell, Coburn, and Chong (2019). They asked, "Under what conditions do school districts learn from external partners?" They studied two departments in an urban school district central office, one that benefitted from professional development and one that did not. As their question suggests, the departments were working with an external professional development provider. And of course, all of the looking at student work professional development we have described in this book, including our own work, was done with an external partner. But we believe that what Farrell and her colleagues discovered may also apply to professional development done internally (e.g., if a school decided to convene PLC groups based in looking at student work).

Farrell and colleagues (2019, p. 955) identified a characteristic they called "absorptive capacity"—that is, the department or district's capacity to absorb, grow, and benefit from the new knowledge and skills generated by the professional development. Absorptive capacity affects interactions with the external professional development provider (or, perhaps, with the internal PLC leaders), which in turn affects learning outcomes for the teachers involved, including changes in practice. Absorptive capacity has three ingredients: prior knowledge, communication pathways, and strategic leadership knowledge. Prior knowledge means someone in the relevant department or district needs to have some understanding of formative assessment and, in this case, looking at student work. This aspect of a district administrator's role parallels the building administrator's role as a leading learner. Communication pathways means there are regular opportunities for communication about the initiative—in this case, looking at student work. Strategic leadership knowledge encompasses the ability to identify and assess current sources of knowledge available within and outside the district and bring those resources to bear as needed—in this case, to support the PLCs looking at student work.

In all, support from school and district leaders is critical if teachers are to make the shifts in mindset, knowledge, and practice that will come with looking at student work in a PLC. Without their support, efforts may founder or be confined to a few individuals. With their support, looking at student work will help teachers and administrators better understand the minds of learners and grow their capacity to cultivate them.

 ## Summary

We hope we have convinced you that looking at student work supports powerful professional learning for teachers and leads to benefits for students, like receiving thoughtful feedback and targeted instruction, as well. We intended our examples to illustrate not only the concepts in each chapter but also how interesting it is to focus squarely on our collective main purpose in schools: what the students are doing and learning. We commend this work and predict that you will love it. We also expect that, if you look at student work collaboratively and with a focus on both teacher and student learning, good things will happen. You will focus on student thinking more than correctness. You will improve the quality of the feedback you give your students. You will plan and implement more targeted next instructional moves. And, if you are like the teachers we worked with, you will enjoy the professional learning you do with colleagues. Let us know. We would love to hear about it!

 ## Reflection Question

We only have one: Now that you have read this book, what are you going to do next?

References

Andrade, H. L., & Brookhart, S. M. (2020). Assessment as the co-regulation of learning. *Assessment in Education: Principles, Policy and Practice, 27*(4), 350–372.

Beesley, A. D., Clark, T. F., Dempsey, K., & Tweed A. (2018). Improving formative assessment practice and encouraging middle school mathematics engagement and persistence. *School Science and Mathematics, 118*(1–2), 4–16.

Blythe, T., Allen, D., & Powell, B. S. (2015). *Looking together at student work* (3rd ed.). New York: Teachers College Press.

Box, C., Skoog, G., & Dabbs, J. M. (2015). A case study of teacher personal practice assessment theories and complexities of implementing formative assessment. *American Educational Research Journal, 52*(5), 956–983.

Brookhart, S. M. (2013). *How to create and use rubrics for formative assessment and grading.* Alexandria, VA: ASCD.

Brookhart, S. M. (2014). *How to design questions and tasks to assess student thinking.* Alexandria, VA: ASCD.

Brookhart, S. M. (2017). *How to give effective feedback to your students* (2nd ed.). Alexandria, VA: ASCD.

Brookhart, S. M., & Moss, C. M. (2013). Leading by learning. *Phi Delta Kappan, 94*(8), 13–17.

Cleaves, W., & Mayrand, S. (2011). What were they thinking? A closer look at student work in mathematics learning communities. In P. E. Noyce & D. T. Hickey (Eds.), *New frontiers in formative assessment* (pp. 33–48). Cambridge, MA: Harvard Education Press.

Dempsey, K., Beesley, A., Clark, T. F., & Tweed, A. (2015). Authentic student work samples support formative assessment in middle school. In C. Suurtamm & A. R. McDuffie (Eds.), *Annual perspectives in mathematics education 2015: Assessment to enhance learning and teaching* (pp. 157–166). Reston, VA: National Council of Teachers of Mathematics.

Dempsey, K., Beesley, A. D., Clark, T. F., & Tweed A. (2016). Empowering students as partners in learning. In M. Murphy, S. Redding, & J. S. Twyman (Eds.), *Handbook on personalized learning for states, districts, and schools* (pp. 89–97). Philadelphia: Center on Innovations in Learning. Retrieved from https://files.eric.ed.gov/fulltext/ED568173.pdf

Easton, L. B. (2009). *Protocols for professional learning*. Alexandria, VA: ASCD.

Farrell, C. C., Coburn, C. E., & Chong, S. (2019). Under what conditions do school districts learn from external partners? The role of absorptive capacity. *American Educational Research Journal, 56*(3), 955–994.

Furtak, E. M., Circi, R., & Heredia, S. C. (2018). Exploring alignment among learning progressions, teacher-designed formative assessment tasks, and student growth: Results of a four-year study. *Applied Measurement in Education, 31*(2), 143–156.

Furtak, E. M., Kiemer, K., Circi, R. K., Swanson, R., de León, V., Morrison, D., & Heredia, S. C. (2016). Teachers' formative assessment abilities and their relationship to student learning: Findings from a four-year intervention study. *Instructional Science, 44*(3), 267–291.

Gearhart, M., Nagashima, S., Pfotenhauer, J., Clark, S., Schwab, C., Vendlinski, T., Osmundson, E., Herman, J., & Bernbaum, D. J. (2006). Developing expertise with classroom assessment in K–12 science: Learning to interpret student work. Interim findings from a two-year study. *Educational Assessment, 11*(3 & 4), 237–263.

Hattie, J., & Timperley, H. (2007). The power of feedback. *Review of Educational Research, 77*(1), 81–112.

Heritage, M. (2008). *Learning progressions: Supporting instruction and formative assessment*. Washington, DC: Council of Chief State School Officers.

Heritage, M., & Heritage, J. (2013). Teacher questioning: The epicenter of instruction and assessment. *Applied Measurement in Education, 26*(3), 176–190.

Heritage, M., Kim, J., Vendlinski, T., & Herman, J. (2009). From evidence to action: A seamless process in formative assessment? *Educational Measurement: Issues and Practice, 28*(3), 24–31.

Heritage, M., & Wylie, E. C. (2020). *Formative assessment in the disciplines: Framing a continuum of professional learning*. Cambridge, MA: Harvard Education Press.

Kazemi, E., & Franke, M. L. (2004). Teacher learning in mathematics: Using student work to promote collective inquiry. *Journal of Mathematics Teacher Education, 7*(3), 203–235.

Langer, G. M., Colton, A. B., & Goff, L. S. (2003). *Collaborative analysis of student work: Improving teaching and learning*. Alexandria, VA: ASCD.

Lee, H., Chung, H. Q., Zhang, Y., Abedi, J., & Warschauer, M. (2020). The effectiveness and features of formative assessment in US K–12 education: A systematic review. *Applied Measurement in Education, 33*(2), 124–140.

Leighton, J. (2019). Cognitive demand is not enough: The challenge of measuring learning with classroom assessments. In S. M. Brookhart & J. H. McMillan (Eds.), *Classroom assessment and educational measurement* (pp. 27–45). New York: Routledge.

Little, J. W., Gearhart, M., Curry, M., & Kafka, J. (2003). Looking at student work for teacher learning, teacher community, and school reform. *Phi Delta Kappan, 85*(3), 184–192.

Massachusetts Department of Elementary and Secondary Education. (2011). *Mathematics learning community overview: Facilitator materials.* Worcester, MA: Regional Science Center of the University of Massachusetts Medical School.

Moss, C. M., & Brookhart, S. M. (2012). *Learning targets: Helping students aim for understanding in today's lesson.* Alexandria, VA: ASCD.

Moss, C. M., & Brookhart, S. M. (2019). *Advancing formative assessment in every classroom: A guide for instructional leaders* (2nd ed.). Alexandria, VA: ASCD.

NAEP (National Assessment of Educational Progress). (n.d.). *NAEP questions tool.* https://nces.ed.gov/nationsreportcard/data/

NCDPI (North Carolina Department of Public Instruction). (n.d.). *K–12 standards, curriculum, and instruction.* Retrieved from https://sites.google.com/dpi.nc.gov/k-12-sci/

Otero, V. K. (2006). Moving beyond the "get it or don't" conception of formative assessment. *Journal of Teacher Education, 57*(3), 247–255.

Ruiz-Primo, M. A., & Brookhart, S. M. (2018). *Using feedback to improve learning.* New York: Routledge.

Ruiz-Primo, M. A., Kroog, H. I., & Sands, D. I. (2015, August). *Teacher judgments on-the-fly: Teachers' response patterns in the context of informal formative assessment.* Paper presented at the EARLI Biennial Conference, Limassol, Cyprus.

Ruiz-Primo, M. A., & Li, M. (2013). Analyzing teachers' feedback practices in response to students' work in a science classroom. *Applied Measurement in Education, 26*(3), 163–175.

Sadler, D. R. (1989). Formative assessment and the design of instructional systems. *Instructional Science, 18*(2), 119–144.

Schneider, M. C., & Gowan, P. (2013). Investigating teachers' skills in interpreting evidence of student learning. *Applied Measurement in Education, 26*(3), 191–204.

Schneider, M. C., & Randel, B. (2010). Research on characteristics of effective professional development programs for enhancing educators' skills in formative assessment. In H. L. Andrade & G. J. Cizek (Eds.), *Handbook of formative assessment* (pp. 251–276). New York: Routledge.

Steinberg, R. M., Empson, S. B., & Carpenter, T. P. (2004). Inquiry into children's mathematical thinking as a means to teacher change. *Journal of Mathematics Teacher Education, 7*(3), 237–267.

Trumbull, E., & Gerzon, N. (2013). *Professional development on formative assessment: Insights from research and practice.* San Francisco: WestEd. Retrieved from https://www.wested.org/resources/professional-development-on-formative-assessment-insights-from-research-and-practice/

Windschitl, M., Thompson, J., & Braaten, M. (2011). Ambitious pedagogy by novice teachers: Who benefits from tool-supported collaborative inquiry into practice and why? *Teachers College Record, 113*(7), 1311–1360.

Winstone, N. E., Nash, R. A., Parker, M., & Rowntree, J. (2017). Supporting learners' agentic engagement with feedback: A systematic review and a taxonomy of recipience processes. *Educational Psychologist, 52*(1), 17–37.

Index

The letter *f* following a page number denotes a figure.

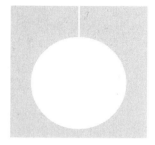

About the Authors

Susan M. Brookhart, PhD, is professor emerita in the School of Education at Duquesne University and an independent educational consultant and author based in Los Angeles, California. She was the 2007–2009 editor of *Educational Measurement: Issues and Practice* and is currently an associate editor of *Applied Measurement in Education*. She is author or coauthor of 20 books and more than 80 articles and book chapters on classroom assessment, teacher professional development, and evaluation. She has been named the 2014 Jason Millman Scholar by the Consortium for Research on Educational Assessment and Teaching Effectiveness (CREATE) and is the recipient of the 2015 Samuel J. Messick Memorial Lecture Award from ETS/TOEFL. Brookhart's research interests include the role of both formative and summative classroom assessment in student motivation and achievement, the connection between classroom assessment and large-scale assessment, and grading. She also works with schools, districts, regional educational service units, universities, and states doing professional development. Brookhart received her PhD in educational research and evaluation from The Ohio State University, after teaching in both elementary and middle schools. She can be reached at brookhart@duq.edu.

 **Alice Oakley** cofounded Education Resource Group (ERG) in 2004. Its mission is to provide high-quality staff development services that promote the growth of all learners. A lifelong educator, Oakley has taught elementary, middle, and high school classes including science, social studies, and English language arts. She was also a curriculum facilitator at the school level and then moved to the district office to be part of the formative assessment team. Since cofounding ERG, Oakley has coached adults and led professional development in a variety of preK–12 settings. As a National Board Certified Teacher, she has developed materials for classroom teachers, instructional leaders, administrators, and parents on a variety of academic topics, instructional methods, and human behaviors. Oakley has a bachelor's degree in early and middle grades education from Radford University and a master's degree in curriculum and instruction from the University of North Carolina at Greensboro. She can be reached at alice@myedresource.com.

Related ASCD Resources: Assessment

At the time of publication, the following resources were available (ASCD stock numbers in parentheses).

Advancing Formative Assessment in Every Classroom: A Guide for Instructional Leaders, 2nd Edition by Connie M. Moss and Susan M. Brookhart (#120005)

Assessing with Respect: Everyday Practices That Meet Students' Social and Emotional Needs by Starr Sackstein (#121023)

Checking for Understanding: Formative Assessment Techniques for Your Classroom, 2nd Edition by Douglas Fisher and Nancy Frey (#115011)

Facilitating Teacher Teams and Authentic PLCs: The Human Side of Leading People, Protocols, and Practices by Daniel R. Venables (#117004)

Giving Students a Say: Smarter Assessment Practices to Empower and Engage by Myron Dueck (#119013)

How to Create and Use Rubrics for Formative Assessment and Grading by Susan M. Brookhart (#112001)

How to Design Questions and Tasks to Assess Student Thinking by Susan M. Brookhart (#114014)

How to Give Effective Feedback to Your Students, 2nd Edition by Susan M. Brookhart (#116066)

How to Make Decisions with Different Kinds of Student Assessment Data by Susan M. Brookhart (#116003)

How Teachers Can Turn Data into Action by Daniel R. Venables (#114007)

How to Use Grading to Improve Learning by Susan M. Brookhart (#117074)

Learning Targets: Helping Students Aim for Understanding in Today's Lesson by Connie M. Moss and Susan M. Brookhart (#112002)

What We Know About Grading: What Works, What Doesn't, and What's Next by Thomas R. Guskey and Susan M. Brookhart (#118062)

For up-to-date information about ASCD resources, go to www.ascd.org. You can search the complete archives of *Educational Leadership* at www.ascd.org/el.

ASCD myTeachSource®

Download resources from a professional learning platform with hundreds of research-based best practices and tools for your classroom at http://myteachsource .ascd.org/

For more information, send an e-mail to member@ascd.org; call 1-800-933-2723 or 703-578-9600; send a fax to 703-575-5400; or write to Information Services, ASCD, 1703 N. Beauregard St., Alexandria, VA 22311-1714 USA.